I'mperfect As I Am

Break free from the prison of perfectionism to a whole new level of **Self-love**, **Self-acceptance** and **Self-confidence**

I'mperfect As I Am

Break free from the
prison of perfectionism
to a whole new level of
Self-love,
Self-acceptance and
Self-confidence

WENDY FELICITY FIRMIN-PRICE

Copyright © 2022 by Wendy Felicity Firmin-Price

All rights reserved. No part of this book may be used or reproduced in any manner whatsoever without prior written consent of the authors, except as provided by the United States of America copyright law.

Published by Best Seller Publishing®, St. Augustine, FL
Best Seller Publishing® is a registered trademark.
Printed in the United States of America.
ISBN: 978-1-956649-37-6

This publication is designed to provide accurate and authoritative information with regard to the subject matter covered. It is sold with the understanding that the publisher is not engaged in rendering legal, accounting, or other professional advice. If legal advice or other expert assistance is required, the services of a competent professional should be sought. The opinions expressed by the authors in this book are not endorsed by Best Seller Publishing® and are the sole responsibility of the author rendering the opinion.

For more information, please write:
Best Seller Publishing®
53 Marine Street
St. Augustine, FL 32084
or call 1 (626) 765-9750
Visit us online at: www.BestSellerPublishing.org

Table of Contents

Acknowledgements ix
Introduction 1
CHAPTER 1: The Prison of Perfectionism............................... 9
CHAPTER 2: Your Perfect Mirror — Your Imperfect Reflection 21
CHAPTER 3: The Emotional Effects of Not Feeling Perfect............. 31
CHAPTER 4: Failure, Fear and Other Flawed Feelings 45
CHAPTER 5: Change the Self Script 59
CHAPTER 6: Rooting Out the Causes 69
CHAPTER 7: Letting Go of the Reins of Control 81
CHAPTER 8: The Silent Saboteur of Success 89
CHAPTER 9: Let Go of the Past to Free Yourself for the Future 101
CHAPTER 10: The Gift of the Present 111
CHAPTER 11: Finding the Perfect Solution in the Imperfect Situation 119
CHAPTER 12: The Tasks Before You Are Never Greater Than the Power Behind You!.. 129

I dedicate this book to my ever-supportive husband, John, who truly loves and accepts me Imperfectly as I am.

Acknowledgements

To all my teachers, students, clients, staff, family, friends (and seeming foes) who have made this transformational journey of my life possible.

I especially am in gratitude to all my horses who give so much in service to me and my clients.

Thank you.

Introduction

If only I were ...

Someone I once knew ...

Sixty-two years old, sixty-two pounds overweight and at least sixty-two projects, courses, expensive programmes unfinished, or sitting in my inbox, forgotten they had even been purchased. My library was full of 'shelf-help' books, unread or unfinished. I had come to a full stop, exhausted, burnt out and deflated. Everything I had worked for in my life seemed a complete and utter disaster and a total waste of time. As I lay in the darkened room, my body feeling paralysed with fear and unable to move, I started to seriously question my ability to carry on with my life. The pain of feeling such a failure was agonising. I felt like a frog in free fall, with nothing and no one there to catch me.

Fed up with having to hide my deep depression and live an upbeat life, always jollying along others and being the positive one, I felt such a fraud. I was convinced that if people knew what was really going on with me, they wouldn't hire me, like me or respect me anymore. I would lose so much face, people would think less of me. I would be totally exposed.

The thought of that humiliation was too overwhelming; the feeling of shame should that happen coursed through every vein in my body. *I was supposed to be the one with all the answers; I was the one spouting* peace, love and harmony; *I* was the one saying 'feel your feelings', yet this inner rage, despair, sadness and apathy I was experiencing had all consumed me, in more ways than one.

As a therapeutic coach and HEART equine-assisted therapist, I spent my days creating the bridge between letting go of the past and creating the future my clients desired.

'For things to change, you need to change your thinking', I'd counsel. 'Bring your vibrational energy up to that which you desire and act as if you already have it'.

'Find the next-level feeling', I would lovingly coach. Blah blah blah.

Ironically, what was even more frustrating was that the people I coached were getting amazing manifestations happening. I was a master at helping people find the origin of their limiting beliefs that they had taken on innocently as children and transform their earlier programming that was causing havoc in their lives. I was making their dreams come true. Meanwhile, I was caught in a terrifying nightmare I couldn't wake up from. The debts were piling up, the pounds were piling on and my excuses were piling in.

The feelings of failure, not being good enough and totally useless, kept me from asking for help. I was way too proud, too independent and just too downright stubborn to seek proper support.

I had spent thousands on courses, mentors and advertising to help my business, believing that if I just knew this, or overcame that, I could prove I was good enough and then clients would want me. Everything was done in a desperate attempt to get it right, to prove I was worthy enough, and yet everything I tried backfired, or I sabotaged or just simply failed at. I told myself, 'You just need to be more perfect, do "it/everything" more perfectly or just find a way to feel faultless'.

When you feel like you are hanging on by your fingernails, could this be the time to just surrender? Maybe it is better to just let go and experience the pain of the fall. Unfortunately, once you do find yourself at the bottom of this massive chasm, it is really hard to find traction on the cliff edges to get back up. Nonetheless, the great thing about being at your rock bottom is that you can't get any lower, and so it is, finally and ironically, a place where you can rest, recover and rethink your life.

Now, it is one thing to have the luxury of going through this pity potty party if it is just yourself you have to think of, but what about when you are responsible for a family, kids, pets, running a business, clients' welfare and, in my case, more than thirty horses?

The problem? I was suffering from im-perfectionism. Nothing ever was right, good enough or perfect enough. Now some people call that perfectionism, but if you are only ever looking at what is wrong, I prefer to call it im-perfectionism.

This summed up my life as I was writing this book. Talk about research! I certainly wasn't feeling good enough about myself. I had a PhD in im-perfectionism, procrastination and self-persecution.

I frequently lamented, 'What's the point, nothing is ever going to change'.

I had the Oscar in hiding the imposter syndrome. I was feeling such a fake. 'If I can't make a difference, and if with all my qualifications and experience I can't create what I really want, what right do I have to teach others how to manifest or change their life?' I moaned.

I was the perpetual student, always trying to learn where I was going wrong. Worse than that, I was suffering from the secret sabotage syndrome as well. Every time I got ahead, especially financially, I would 'create' yet another vet bill, or something would go wrong with the tractors, or clients would cancel at the last moment and refuse to pay the cancellation fee. It didn't matter how much money I manifested; my harsh saboteur made sure I had so many holes in my pockets that it just poured through. My efforts felt like I was trying to fill a container with a colander. To my inner saboteur, nothing I ever did would be good enough, and it certainly made sure of that! I can't describe the depths of that emotional torture I felt, as if I were putting myself through hell.

Have you ever had that feeling where, right in the core of your being, you feel so bad, so broken, so helpless that nothing ever seems to go well? As if someone has locked you in a cell and thrown away the key and you are to serve this lifelong sentence with no parole?

Well take heart, I did find the key. I did break free from that prison, and I did get that lifelong sentence overturned. I gained an inner freedom that allowed true peace and prosperity, and everything working out perfectly.

What is *I'mperfect As I Am* all about?

If you have ever felt something similar, this is the journey back to feeling good enough — just as you are. From reading this book, you'll discover a way to break free from this relentless, punishing and unkind way to live and instead take yourself to a whole new level of unconditional self-love, self-acceptance and the confidence to be yourself. This is the map to find perfection in what goes wrong. Here are the road signs to point you back to truth. Your Inner Satnav will not only show you the importance of approving of yourself just the way you are but also how.

The true reality is that you are good enough just the way you are. You are already perfect. You don't have to change you per se; you just need to change your perspective of you. When you are born, you know only unconditional love in that moment, but then as you develop, you take on mistaken beliefs about yourself. Certain events happen which you interpret to mean you must not be loveable. Maybe being yourself got you into trouble. Or even more commonly, you may have erroneously believed you were to blame for why x y z happened. These beliefs will be like apps, still running in the background today, slowing your life down. You need your neck-top computer programming uninstalled and a new upgraded version uploaded.

Why?

Because until you have rediscovered that unconditional love and acceptance for who you are, as you are, warts and all — you will never experience true peace and contentment. There will always be a relentless need to keep proving you are perfect, or to look perfect enough or that you must have the perfect life. There will be an emptiness that no amount of perfection, food, drugs, drink or other addictions or distractions can fill. It is time to stop blaming yourself, punishing yourself or believing there must be something wrong with you. Freedom lies on the other side of this prison sentence.

I don't know anyone who hasn't gone through not feeling good enough at some time in their life. Sometimes you may not even realise that that belief system is in operation, especially if you are one of those people demanding perfection from yourself and others. By the time you have read this book, I hope to have helped you uncover the hidden beliefs, behaviours or blocks to your self-acceptance, self-love and self-confidence.

Not Just an Adult Thing

One of the saddest things I have witnessed in my increasing years is the number of children growing up with social anxiety. Rather than social media creating a place of connection and friendship, it is often the source of cyberbullying, body-shaming, body competition, who can be the thinnest, muscly-est, prettiest, poutiest and so on. Alarmingly, even self-harming has become a competition of who can show the most cuts, be in the most pain or have the biggest drama. Even their emotional pain is not expressed authentically.

The level of broken families, self-harming, addictions, acting out, self-deprecation, mental health problems and behavioural challenges is almost immeasurable. This has led to masses of people suffering the loss of confidence. We unconsciously sabotage our success through procrastination or the impossible task of trying to be perfect.

The result? Massive loss of potential, feelings of failure, perfectionism, debt, depression, illnesses, absenteeism, lost dreams and, at worst, suicide. Stress-related illnesses all stem from feeling not good enough.

I have spent six decades desperately trying to feel worthy and justify my existence. For years I tried to get people's approval, see my value and appreciate me for being me. To say I was a people-pleaser was an understatement. There is nothing wrong in wanting to please others, but when you do it at the cost of displeasing yourself, it soon takes its toll, one way or another. I could never believe I was good enough.

Finally, I realised, with the help of difficult life events, what a futile strategy perfectionism was, and it's my hope for you that if this has been a pattern for you, too, this book will give you some clues on how to find true peace and perfection. Maybe I can save you years of fruitless activity.

I truly feel for you if you are still in that deep place of despair, depression or feeling dejected, believing you can't get it right no matter how hard you try. I can relate to that black hole you may be in. I trust that my own journey through one will give you some new tools to build the path back to sanity. I would love it if you'd allow me to share with you some ideas on how to break that cycle and give you back your life so that once again you can feel confident, calm and capable. Let me show you your true perfection — just as you are. Please take what fits for YOUR truth and your map of the world and leave the rest.

Only when we know the truth of our being can we experience true peace, true love and true perfection.
—WENDYISM

I may have all the theoretical proof of internationally accredited coaching certificates, letters after my name and numerous qualifications. I pioneered equine-assisted therapy in the U.K. thirty years ago. I have therapeutically coached thousands of clients, but what I really offer as my credentials are my life experiences and being the living proof that no matter where you find yourself in life, going through the deepest valley or darkest night of the soul, there is a way out. Let me shine the light and give you the key to get out of this prison.

Perfectly Imperfect

The sooner you realise the real dichotomy of perfectionism, the sooner you can relax and enjoy the ride. Yes, it is good you want to strive for excellence, be the best you can, but when you cannot bear to fail or bear the slightest thing going wrong or not being right, then maybe you are missing the more spiritual meaning of perfection. This is where you find the wrong out of the right, the good out of the bad, the perfection out of the imperfection. Only when you can truly STOP judging something, someone and especially yourself as imperfect or not good enough will you find true peace. You are perfectly imperfect.

It's the flaw that makes perfection = I'mperfection. When you can love yourself — the good, the bad AND the ugly — just the way you are, it becomes easy peasy lemon squeezy to love everyone else.

In 2017 there was a major fire at my stables where I have more than thirty horses. It happened in the middle of the night. Naturally, I hadn't wanted that to happen, but again the reality was that it did.

Odd as it may sound, all I could experience the day after was extreme gratitude.

Gratitude for my neighbour ringing me when she heard the explosion. And gratitude for my neighbour also then running at five o'clock in the morning straight to the stables to release any trapped horses.

Gratitude for the fact that there were only three or four horses there that night, so we could quickly evacuate.

Gratitude that when the imperfect local water source was not strong enough for the firefighters' hoses, another neighbour very generously let the firefighters use his swimming pool.

Gratitude that the weather had changed from the heat and drought we'd been in and suddenly became cooler, so the horses could stay out while we repaired the stables.

There were numerous 'perfections' out of something so imperfect that eventually created change, improvement and so many blessings.

> *When you get lemons, create lemonade,*
> *and you will soon find your problems fade.*
> —WENDYISM

Self-Love Creates Self-Confidence

The reason you, me, all of us need to increase self-love is that it really will change the world. Imagine the next generation of children learning how to love themselves as they are. What impact would that have? Remember, it starts with you. *I'mperfect As I Am* shows you how to overcome feeling stuck, stressed or dissatisfied so you can live an empowered life filled with ease, energy and enthusiasm — just the way you authentically are.

CHAPTER 1

The Prison of Perfectionism

Life is like a clump of clay:
You can get stuck in it, sling mud at yourself,
or mould it to your desire.

—WENDYISM

Sitting in her uninviting cell, surrounded by a barrage of bullies, the bombardment of verbal abuse was relentless.

'You stupid idiot, you should have known better. How could you be such a clot?' they jeered.

'Why bother, you will only fail … What will they think of you now?' they taunted.

'Why would anyone want to choose you? You are not good enough', they jeered.

'It had better be absolutely perfect; otherwise you will get rejected', they warned.

'What is the point of starting? You will only get it wrong!' they hissed.

Why was no one stepping in and stopping this attacking audience? Surely these people should be arrested and put in jail for the way they were browbeating this poor person. Why was this person even allowing the abuse? Why was this person not standing up for themselves?

Take a moment and reread.

Does it possibly sound familiar?

Where have you heard something similar?

Could it be from the hecklers in *your* head, too?

The suffocating world of self-attack, self-deprecation and lack of self-love sadly is fast becoming a very real mental health issue. The consequences of holding such devastating dialogues with yourself is that it can lead to unhelpful coping strategies like addictions, debt, disease, depression, dysfunctional relationships and many other stressful sabotaging symptoms. These and more destructive behaviours are designed to distract from the overwhelming feelings of inadequacy and the vicious circle of perfectionism or its sidekick, procrastination, that you are likely to be caught up in.

Why Is Self-Love Replaced with Such Self-Loathing?

We are so exposed by the media in all its forms, constantly displaying images of people desperately trying to prove they have the perfect body, the perfect life, the perfect home, the perfect partner, the perfect diet, the perfect business strategy. Billions are spent on the 'bigger, better, best' culture. On the surface, this seeking of perfection seems admirable, but upon deeper investigation, the lack of sincere self-approval lurks behind the pain of feeling imperfect or not good enough. Self-acceptance seems unacceptable unless every flaw has been eradicated. The exterior looks self-loving, but is it really hiding the depths of self-loathing?

Why should it matter what is going on in the hidden world of your own head? These are *your* thoughts, so surely you are entitled to think what you like.

Consider this.

Pretend for a moment that, instead of being a single body, you are part of a whole body. Imagine you are one of the trillions of cells circulating within that body. What if, as that cell, every attacking thought you have makes your cell toxic? Would you agree that toxicity would likely affect the cells next to you? As the attacking thoughts increase, all the cells around it become toxic too, and those cells cannot help affecting the cells around them. You can see that it would not take long for the whole body to be affected. This is pretty much how cancer forms. So, you see, you may think that it is just you and your thoughts, but in fact because it has been proven scientifically by the likes of Albert Einstein, Stephen Hawking and many mystics that we are all one — and of the same energy — your toxic thought DOES affect others.

Believing you are not good enough not only affects your own physical body but may also affect everybody in your environment. Your partner will feel not good enough and consequently feel they are a failure. A child will feel their parent's lack of self-esteem and often blame themself or start taking on board their parent's belief of unworthiness too.

Consequences of Holding Beliefs of Not Being Good Enough

The implication of self-attack and limiting beliefs that perfectionism creates is enormous, and it doesn't just affect you! Everyone in your environment will be affected in some way.

My days are filled with cantankerous kids, troubled teenagers and stressed parents needing my therapeutic coaching because they are feeling anxious, worried and nervous. They have no confidence, are terrified to take risks and some are so depressed they are self-harming, feeling suicidal or sadly exhibiting other forms of self-destructive behaviour. Many kids are already addicted to medication, iPads or sugar. The underlying belief system behind all their distresses? Not feeling good enough, perfect enough or even just enough.

Where Are the Children Getting It From?

For children to start feeling not good enough, they must be getting it from somewhere. In Chapter 6, we will go into more depth about this, but for now, the key reasons children feel inadequate is that they pick up a lot of mistaken assumptions and beliefs as they grow up and are also affected by the environment they live in. So, if you do not feel good enough as a parent, you can bet your children or others around you are likely to feel that too.

What You Believe You Must Prove

There is a part of your mind that is like the soil. What you sow is what you grow. The soil gives back the evidence of those seeds sown. It is completely impartial. Those 'seeds' are equivalent to your beliefs, which are then returned as experiences to you.

Consequently, when you sow the seeds of not feeling perfect enough, you attract people in your life to evidence this (what you sow is what you grow). You attract people who take advantage of you, reject you and are unlikely to see your value. This is especially apparent if you are in business — it can feel that no matter how hard you try your best, give your best or be your best, it will not be good enough for some of your customers. Clients will not want to pay your true worth. But then, why should they? If you are unable to value yourself, what right do you have to transfer that responsibility to someone else?

Consequently, there is constant striving to look outwardly perfect to hide the inner torture of not feeling good enough, and these behaviours become more and more addictive.

We all need to accept accountability that if we are perfection seekers, we are contributing to the epidemic of not feeling good enough.

Start believing you are good enough as you are right now.

Believe your kids are good enough as they are.

Believe your employees give the best they can.

I am not suggesting to NOT have goals, standards and aspirations, or even to give false praise and acclamation to people who aren't coming up to the mark, but rather acknowledge their effort given and encourage, educate and enthuse. Fundamentally, everything boils down to the beliefs you hold about yourself, others and life. This colours your experience of life.

The only way to reach true perfection is to let yourself out of that prison of perfectionism and love and accept yourself exactly as you are. Only then can you have the true compassion needed to love someone else unconditionally, yet not allow yourself to be affected by behaviours that are less than perfect.

The Lie of Perfectionism

I once worked with a business coach who was exactly the epitome of an 'imperfectionist' (what I call someone who only ever sees what is wrong). She would constantly nitpick at everything. Her favourite expression was 'May I give you feedback?' which was code for 'Can I criticise what you have done?' My energy would immediately slump. The challenge I had was not that I did not have the drive to be better and to excel, which I valued, but to feel I was making progress. However, there was never a time I felt good enough in her presence. Now I recognise that was partly my own stuff, but I never had the feeling that she was pleased with me. I often came away demoralised after what I thought had been done well, only to find out this was wrong, that could have been done better or I should have done it differently somehow.

Perfectionism is the biggest lie because there is no such thing as a so-called perfectionist. There is never a time when it is, was or ever will be perfect enough. To the 'perfectionist', even when they get a 10/10 or A+, they usually attack themselves with a judgement like 'Yes, but it wasn't done quick enough', or they excuse their achievement as lucky or, worse still, even when perfection is reached, there is no rest, no satisfaction, no true peace. There is *always* something that is not right. The perfectionist does not see perfection, so I call them imperfectionists — because they only ever see what is wrong or NOT perfect.

To me, true perfectionism would allow you to find perfection in the imperfection. To find the right in the wrong. Hence the title of this book.

When you work for a perfectionist boss, you very seldom feel you have done a good job, because they want and demand even more perfection. And even if you are proud of what you have achieved, their hidden disappointment or dissatisfaction leaks out of them, and you can't help feeling you should have done better.

Don't get me wrong—if you are being paid to do a job, then your employer has every right to expect a certain standard and result. How you can tell the difference is the way you come away from that meeting or discussion. True positive feedback will help you feel empowered, proud and willing to do more, but subtle attack disguised as feedback will certainly tap into your feelings of not being good enough and you will probably feel very demoralised and less enthusiastic to support them.

Remember, the boss who is the perfectionist and is giving you that type of feedback is secretly feeling desperately low in self-esteem and self-worth too.

Going back to my business coach, I do appreciate that I was paying her for honest feedback; however there was so little positive feedback or even an acknowledgement of the 'try' that I quickly lost the confidence to even attempt anything for fear of reprimand or the look of her disappointed and disapproving face. The consequence of this was that I fell into the paralysis of procrastination, terrified to even start a project because I knew it wouldn't be good enough.

Can you relate to what you are reading?

Perfectionists have deep-rooted terrors of being criticised, of not being good enough or of having their ideas rejected. They are constantly feeling crushed inside when someone remarks how something could have been done differently.

But what about standards; won't they drop?

How can you achieve excellence if you are not seeking perfection? Isn't that a contradiction? Excellence could be perceived as perfectionism, but I personally do not think perfectionism is necessarily excellence. For me, excellence has more of a positive, external energy to it. It has a desire to be of service to others.

One dictionary definition of *excellence* is 'To give of one's best, to go beyond the norm or what is expected'.

For me, it also allows for growth and positive feedback but without that devastating dialogue if not achieved. Using the word *excellence* exudes a feeling of pride and, in the workplace, can produce a productive team much more invested and willing to support.

The boss who seeks excellence rather than perfection is much more likely to say, 'That wasn't quite to the standard I was hoping to deliver; I wonder what we could have done differently?'

The narcissistic perfectionist boss would say 'That was s***. You have messed up and got it wrong'. (Their own inner self-talk would be similar too.)

Now compare this with what the person I define as 'the true perfectionist' might say. The one who is seeking the perfection in the imperfection.

'I wonder how this project going differently to my expectations can serve me? How can I turn this situation to my advantage and make the "wrong" right?!'

Which voice would you prefer? Compare the emotional feeling to each statement.

If we look at more dictionary definitions, 'Excellence means greatness — the absolute best. Achieving excellence is never easy to do. Excellence is a quality that people really appreciate because it is so hard to find. Excellence is the quality of excelling, of being truly the best at something'.

Compare this to the definition of perfectionism: 'Perfectionism: a disposition to regard anything short of perfection as unacceptable; especially the setting of unrealistically demanding goals accompanied by a disposition to regard failure to achieve them as unacceptable and a sign of personal worthlessness'.

Can you see from the two descriptions that one feels exciting, attainable and worth going for, whilst the other is so disheartening, why would you even want to try?

Hence, this is where the 'Perfectionism is the mother of procrastination' statement comes from.

Naturally, when carrying the belief of not being good enough, the impetus to get moving is extremely limited. A common challenge the procrastinator is likely to have is dozens of non-started, unfinished or unread courses, books and projects. The hope is always in the 'If I only knew this better, other people would see me as good enough'.

Or,

'If I get this qualification, then I will feel confident to go forward'.

'I just need to know more about _____, then my business will do better'.

'I just need this information, then I can submit a better project'.

'When I can succeed at this, then I will stop feeling a failure!'

Why are these insane strategies?

Because the person is using everything outside of themselves to find validation.

Their underlying fear is that the feeling of 'not being good enough' will still be there. That, in turn, leads the person to continue putting off what they know they need to do. The belief that it will not be perfect enough, and therefore nor will they be, confirms their hidden dread. By not getting on with things, they have their perfect excuse if they fail.

A pattern of behaviour in me personally that I have had to change is putting off advertising for my workshops well in advance. I was a 'last-minutedotcommer'. When I finally had the courage to examine this pattern, I could see that if no one or only a few people booked, I could use my 'perfect excuse' of advertising too late as a way of consoling myself.

You see, if I advertised well in advance and still only got one or two, that would be worse because it would confirm my deepest dread that I was unlovable and not good enough, and therefore nobody would want me or what I had to offer. It is an insane coping skill, but when the psyche has been so wounded at an early age, the part of you that is trying to look after you will do its best to protect you from ever feeling unwanted, unlovable or hurt again. When you get your real eyes (realise) on, you can see logically the insanity of this coping skill. In Chapter 6, we explore exactly where these strategies come from and how to fix the outdated tactics.

Feeling overwhelmed is a symptom that often goes hand in hand with perfectionism.

The seasoned 'putter-offer' will usually have an ever-increasing 'to-do' list, usually starting another project before completing the ones already started. They generally end up having to fight fires and everything becomes last minute. It drives their long-term strategist and completer colleagues to distraction! Rather than complete something, procrastinators are usually off to seek the next shiny object to make them feel better.

The irony is that the procrastinator is often someone very willing to help, often taking on too many tasks for other people. They usually have a hard time saying no to other people, as the need to be liked or, more importantly, to feel good enough is so great that they seldom take care of their own needs. The more they do for others, the worthier they feel — well, at least for that moment. But then it can be like an addiction: constantly seeking people, situations or ways they can get their 'fix' to feel good enough.

These people are unlikely to be particularly good at managing time. They are either busy, busy, busy trying to fit in an unrealistic number of projects, jobs or activities, or they're paralysed by fear, making them waste time zoning out on computer games, TV or other mindless time-wasting things.

However, it is not really time they need to manage. It is what they expect of themselves within that time. We all have twenty-four hours, and no one can manage or change that time! Not even the richest or most powerful person in the world can stop the clock!

What the overwhelmed procrastinator and unrealistic perfectionist may really be experiencing are ways to.

- avoid deeper unresolved issues, especially trauma
- avoid confronting a person or problem
- stop feeling the fear of getting clear
- try to feel in control
- disguise the big tantrum they might be having
- try to get more energy because they feel so tired
- avoid the fear of rejection

These are just a few possible reasons; what might be yours? Take some time to look at the list above and feel into why you are procrastinating and what might be causing you overwhelm.

More Lies

One of the biggest lies the procrastinators tell themselves is that they are too tired and do not have the energy or the time to do what it is that they need to do.

The actual truth is, it takes MORE energy to NOT do something rather than to just get on and do it. The reason for this is when a job needs doing, your mind creates its own 'to-be-done' list. It keeps that 'app' running in the background, adding all the other jobs needing doing to it. The other little-known fact is not only is it using the energy to remember what needs doing but it is also using the amount of energy needed to do the job! This creates an energy leakage. It is exactly like having loads of tabs open or apps running on your computer or phone — it completely slows down the speed. Your mind is no different. It knows when there is no closure, completion or conclusion.

Exercise: Putting It Off

To illustrate this, think of something you have been putting off. If you were to guess out of 100, with a 'score' of 1= feeling no energy and 100= feeling totally energetic, how much energy you might be leaking out by worrying, putting off or refusing to do what you know needs to be done, what would be the number?

Now imagine going and starting that job. What does your energy feel like out of 100?

Now imagine you are doing the main bulk of it. What does your energy feel like?

Now imagine finally finishing the job. What does your energy feel like now?

What if you cannot get started straight away for valid reasons?

Then keep doing this visualisation exercise. It will help you stay aware of how these differences in energy feel in your body so that you can acquire motivation to get started when the time is right. Remember, it is more exhausting to put off something you know must get done than to just do it.

Dr. Sarah was an extremely intelligent person, in fact one of the brainiest people I knew. She had several degrees in a whole manner of subjects, yet when she came to see me, her lack of self-worth and self-belief totally belied the external picture she portrayed. Her lifelong pursuit of proving she was good enough, especially among her male peers, was an exhausting expedition that resulted in her getting burnt out. Her self-confidence was at an all-time low and she was suffering from imposter syndrome. Despite being massively qualified, she was heavily in debt, and her relationship with her husband and children had deteriorated to detrimental effect.

With my therapeutic coaching we uncovered when her need for perfection first started and examined the pattern behind this relentless requirement to prove she was good enough. By going back to the original moment of choice, we were able to rebalance the roles of her inner personality so they could work with her in a different way. The result was that she was still able to pursue her standards of excellence, but now in a way that allowed her to receive the rewards of her hard work and diligence, not just financially but emotionally too. Although she chose to complete her decision to divorce her husband, who never valued her and was constantly putting her down, she was able to attract a very kind and appreciative partner instead.

You deserve to live an authentic life that allows you to say 'I'mperfect as I am, and so are you!'

> *The Truth is, you are perfect whole and complete,*
> *just the lies of your false beliefs to delete.*
> —WENDYISM

For your free bonus content go to www.imperfectasiam.today

CHAPTER 2

Your Perfect Mirror — Your Imperfect Reflection

You can't change the reflection by changing the mirror.
—WENDYISM

The Laws of Attraction and Reflection

Earlier we explored belief systems and how you'll experience a reality that proves those beliefs correct. Life perfectly reflects to you what you are believing. To expand on understanding how you cocreate your reality is to discover the Law of Attraction AND Reflection. This shows up in how people treat you, how you treat people and the situations you find yourself caught up in. These laws of energy tend to work in tandem, which is the key principle behind magnetising and manifesting things to yourself.

How and Why You Attract the People You Do

Did you know these specific Laws of the Universe totally govern your experiences of life? It is not down to random luck or the gods aligning the planets that you meet certain people at certain times of your life. Understanding these specific Laws of Attraction AND Reflection can help you stop feeling like you are a lottery ticket hoping life will pick you!

In addition to your beliefs and emotions emanating certain vibrations, every single one of us carries a vibration, in the same way that every object and place does. We know this from the theories that Albert Einstein, Stephen Hawking and many other eminent scientists have proven, alongside the theory that when you look at a molecule, its behaviour changes. Scientists also substantiate that everything has a magnetic quality to it. We have all heard the expressions 'like attracts like' and 'opposites attract', although for either of these axioms to be true, that which is alike or opposite must have a similar vibration.

When you learn about your vibration and magnetism, you will discover that everyone in your life is, has been and will be perfect to show you the effect your energy field has on all your thoughts, feelings and behaviours. Your whole outer world is a direct mirror to what is going on inside your head.

Perfect Mirrors

People will reflect exactly what you:

- like about yourself;
- hate about yourself;
- believe about life; or
- where you are off-centre or completely out of balance.

As Within, So Without

However, how you experience your reality may be a distortion of what is really happening. For example, you may think somebody is rejecting you, betraying you or not playing ball, but what if all they are doing is reflecting back to you your beliefs, stories and expectations? Unless they are highly self-aware, these people have little option but to follow the script you are unwittingly assigning them. Very few people have the understanding and awareness to keep themselves from being caught up in someone's script.

To give you an example, you may normally be an easy-going, calm, kind person, yet when you are in a certain person's company, you may find yourself acting completely out of character. You may find yourself getting cross, rude or behaving in an absurd way. The chances are this person's script may be saying something like 'People are rude to me, unkind and can't be trusted'.

Scripts Are Like Beliefs

I was in France with a friend of mine who had lived in Paris for several years, and she was saying how grumpy, brusque and unhelpful people were. Sure enough, when we were at our first brasserie, the waiters practically ignored us, were looking disinterested, hardly made eye contact, definitely didn't smile and it certainly came across that we were an inconvenience to their day. As the day went on, we met more and more of these people. I started to think, 'Wow, they really are moody here in France'.

Then I suggested, for fun, that we change our mutual belief about French people and choose to consider the opposite and believe French people were kind, helpful and generous. Now, if you have been to Paris, you know it is full of brasseries and one of the most common sites is everyone crammed shoulder to shoulder and no such thing as personal body space, so as a twosome to get a table for four in peak busy time is almost unheard of. Yet we did. Not only that, but our waiter was also smiley, helpful and chatty. As our trip continued, we met a shop assistant who, with the most beautiful smile, went personally out of her way to help us with something specific we needed; we were given seats on the busy packed metro (unheard of) and had several more of these pleasant experiences for the rest of the day. Even on my last day, I had busy, rushing Frenchmen offer to carry my cases all the way through the subway to the trains!

> *The surest plan to make a man is, think him so.*
> —JAMES RUSSELL LOWELL

In other words, what you think about someone brings about positive and negative actions. They respond to the labels and scripts you assign them.

Naturally, you can believe everyone is wonderful, but there will be times when they don't act that out. So, what else could be going on? One possibility is they could be showing you a shadow side of yourself, or where you might be out of balance.

It is not by chance, bad luck or cosmic karma that somebody treats you unkindly, takes advantage of you or lets you down. It comes through you choosing to believe something about yourself or others. Through understanding the secret of how molecules change according to how you look at them, you can use that scientific understanding to totally change your life. You can change the behaviour of people by how you choose to see them.

> *You have the perfect people in your life,*
> *To bring you balance of both love and strife.*
> —WENDYISM

Further Understanding of the Laws of Attraction and Reflection

The challenge for a lot of people is that they do not recognise the different parts of themselves. We all tend to have a personality that we reveal to the world. It's normal to try to create the 'perfect persona'. For most of us, we will tend to outwardly portray a perfectly well-behaved, pleasant person.

The problem with that is when you don't love and accept yourself the way you are, (the good, the bad and the ugly) that which you deny about yourself you usually disassociate from and end up projecting that denied aspect on to another. Often what is denied in yourself, you tend to heavily criticise and judge mercilessly in another.

A client friend of mine, Anne, had an alcoholic mum and an abusive father, and experienced an extremely traumatic childhood. When she came to see me, Anne was desperate to change her pattern of attracting dysfunctional relationships. Firstly, what we had to do was peel back all the beliefs she had about herself, focusing particularly on what she disliked, what she had rejected and where she was out of balance.

Next, we needed to dig deep and uproot all the limiting beliefs about relationships she had.

For example:

'Relationships are hard work'.

'Men are abusive'.

'I have to be perfect; otherwise, I will be rejected'.

We then explored where those beliefs that she wasn't good enough originated from and how they affected her life and her tendency to consistently attract abusive men. I invited her to investigate what she felt about herself whilst growing up. Her response was that she realised she held the belief that she couldn't possibly be worthy of love or else her mum wouldn't have drunk so much, and that her dad being so abusive must have been her fault—she must have been doing something wrong as a child. However, she also detected that it was during her childhood where she started her obsessive-compulsive disorder behaviour of trying to be perfect to try to prove she was good enough, especially to her father.

We looked at some of the strategies she had adopted. One of them was to people-please, especially when in a relationship. She confessed she was always like a chameleon, trying to fit in with what her partner wanted, most times at the cost of her own truth and integrity. Her strategy of perfectionism, to try to be so perfect so that she wouldn't get rejected, kicked in big time.

So here we see how her belief system of not being good enough would start the pattern of attracting people to her to 'prove' she wasn't good enough. Remember, whatever you believe MUST be proven true. Unfortunately, her vibration of the belief of not being worthy, loveable or good enough could not fail but to draw to her men and situations that would treat her accordingly. Those self-concepts would have to be mirrored back to her by the way others treated her.

But that is not the only reason.

I also invited Anne to explore how these abusive people could be reflecting how SHE was treating herself.

Now, when you take on beliefs as a child that you can't be good enough, or it must be your fault, you will naturally attract someone who is going to act out those beliefs. Not only will they show you what you are believing but also how you are treating yourself. If you are constantly beating up and attacking yourself, can you see how the Laws of Attraction and Reflection would HAVE to attract someone who shows you that by behaving like it too? The Laws of Attraction and Reflection are absolutely precise.

'Help, I'm Living with a Perfectionist!'

When, deep inside, you don't feel good enough, the chances are you will meet your perfect mirror, except that they may be the one acting out the perfectionist programming. Remember, the perfectionist secretly never feels good enough and there is seldom a time when anything will be good enough or perfect enough.

Living with someone like that is so demoralising. For men, if you have a perfectionist partner, the chances are you feel very emasculated by them. For women, you are made to doubt yourself and nothing is ever right or good enough.

Either way, the person acting out the perfectionism will probably be doing things like micromanaging their partner, always offering feedback (which translates to 'let me tell you what you did wrong'), is frequently in control dramas or power struggles and is usually very volatile. Nothing is ever good enough, and you are left feeling disempowered, controlled or being treated like a child.

To the person not feeling good enough about themselves already, they will come away feeling demoralised, deflated and definitely resentful.

Unfortunately, this can then lead to illnesses, major accidents, money problems, career sabotages and, of course, affairs, divorces and separation. The person who never feels good enough for their partner will inevitably go looking elsewhere for validation. Alternatively, they live in fear that their partner will seek perfection elsewhere.

Often people think that changing partners, jobs or geographic location will change the situation, but, as the saying goes, wherever you go, there you are.

Now unfortunately, when you don't resolve something within one relationship, you carry that unresolved issue to the next. Only this time you will probably get to play the part you have just judged and rejected, or your new mirror will exaggerate the part you are denying. And so a pattern begins that becomes extremely hard to break because every time you have a disastrous relationship with someone, you embed the belief that you have been emitting. And so it goes on.

Thirty years ago, I experienced the effect that suppressed and disassociated feelings have on who you attract in relationships. Outwardly, I thought I had met an absolutely charming, adoring partner. He traditionally wooed me with chocolates and flowers. I was soon hooked, feeling grateful (and relieved) that someone found me loveable.

Then change crept in. Initially, I thought my partner just liked to have a drink or two, but it wasn't long before I realised those one or two drinks turned into three or four, then five or six. And then the behaviour started to change. The once fun, loving romantic turned into an aggressive, violent ogre! Always the next day there would be huge remorse, begging for forgiveness, promises of it never happening again. More flowers and chocolates. 'Okay, give him the benefit of the doubt', I reasoned, 'after all, it's only inanimate objects broken'. Then the violence turned physical. In my desperate need to be loved, I readily accepted the 'it was an accident; I didn't mean to hit you' excuses. My arrogant belief was that if only I could love him more, be more of a perfect partner, he would be able to give up the drink. Surely, I must have meant more to him than the alcohol?

I rang Alcoholics Anonymous for help. I'll never forget that phone call because I remember how indignant and offended I felt when they said I needed to go to Al-Anon — the 12-step programme for people affected by alcoholism. I wasn't the one with the problem! Or was I?

Reluctantly I went along, and, sure enough, I was shown where I colluded or enabled the problem to continue. Just at this time, I was also given the book *You Can Heal Your Life* by the wonderful late Louise Hay. You can imagine my reaction to the first chapter, 'You Create Your Own Reality'. *What a load of bunkum*, I thought. If that was true, who in their right mind would choose a reality like mine? Second chapter, 'People Are Your Reflection!' Now it's time to throw the book out! 'There is NO WAY I am like him', I remember defiantly declaring.

Or was there?

How can this raging, violent alcoholic, who stole, lied and cheated, be me? I never get angry; I am a Miss Goody Two-shoes! Naturally, I protested there was NO WAY I could possibly be like him. I was honest, calm, kind.

Yes, to the outside world I was. But inwardly, the amount of self-attack was enormous; in fact, if the authorities were able to 'hear' my inner critics, I am sure I would have been arrested for bullying and treating myself so cruelly. I was so disassociated from my anger I had to attract someone who showed me EXACTLY what rage I was really carrying. I didn't steal from people or lie to them, but I sure robbed myself of self-esteem and lived a lie.

Okay, I wasn't an alcoholic, but addictions don't just come in the form of alcohol, drugs and gambling. There were many areas of my life where I was addicted to something — debts, food, smoking, dysfunctional relationships!

Eventually, I reluctantly realised that my violent partner was the shadow part of me that I had denied, disassociated from and which kept me in dysfunctional relationships. Something (or rather I) had to change.

So, how do you change these patterns?

Exercise: Judgement Day!

List all the judgements you have:

- of people in general
- of someone significant
- of yourself

Now think of judgements other people have of you.

Next, explore where might you be like that, where do you exhibit the same trait (although maybe not necessarily in the same way). Now investigate where you do that to yourself.

Now you recognise that each and every one of us is like a great big disco ball with thousands of facets, and that all of us have the good, the bad and the ugly somewhere inside.

Just for a moment, get very honest with yourself.

Where HAVE you judged someone to be not as good as you? The tramp on the street? The person whose home isn't as tidy as yours? The colleague at work who doesn't come up to your standards? How about the person who is too fat/too thin, in your opinion? I must confess, I struggle with a particular English accent that really grates on me when I hear it used. How many times do you judge someone by the way they look? Or talk? Or their profession?

If you really are a Goody Two-shoes and have no judgement on others (I've never found anyone in more than fifty years who didn't judge), how do you judge yourself? Where do you feel superior to others, or even to your own personality?

Accordingly, we have over 5,000 traits within each of us. So we have a lot of integrating to do! And that is why the people who press your buttons the most are secretly there to help you learn how to love and accept yourself unconditionally — all of you.

For your free bonus content go to www.imperfectasiam.today

CHAPTER 3

The Emotional Effects of Not Feeling Perfect

When you feel it, you can heal it!

— WENDYISM

So far, we have explored how and why you attract certain people into your life and touched on how you create your reality. In this chapter, we identify how these hurtful beliefs, scripts and stories you tell yourself create myriad emotions and feelings. Unhealed or unexpressed, these feelings get stuck in your body and lead to distress, depression, disease and even debt.

This in turn leads to the use of further behaviours and strategies to cope, such as addictions, workaholism, acting out and self-harming. Stuck emotions and feelings affect finances, health, career, relationships and self-esteem and so on.

This chapter offers you the perfect antidote to these behaviours and shares with you how to embrace your emotions effectively to develop your emotional intelligence and therefore achieve happier outcomes. Practical and yet simple scientific energy tools can help shift years of built-up toxicity that have come about from feeling not good enough.

Emotions create an energetic vibration that drives perfectionism and procrastination.

We have come to understand from Albert Einstein and Stephen Hawking that everything is energy, and that energy creates vibrations. These vibrations are magnetic and emit a frequency, and that like-energy/frequency attracts like-energy. This is particularly true of emotions. Every emotion (energy in motion) has a certain frequency. Another way of understanding this is to pop a glass of water on the table and play different types of music. You will observe the vibrations change depending on the music that is being played. Humans are made of mostly water and so respond to those outside factors to give us different vibrations too.

Vibrational Frequency of Feelings and Emotions

FREQUENCY HZ	EMOTIONAL STATE	DESCRIPTION
700-1000	ENLIGHTENMENT	Powerful inspiration
650	GRATITUDE	The feeling of being grateful for the good, the bad and the ugly
600	PEACE	Calm within the storm
540	JOY	Effortless happiness
500	LOVE	Purity of motive from the heart
400	REASON	Intelligence, rationality and knowledge
350	ACCEPTANCE	Major transformation now possible
310	WILLINGNESS	Overcoming inner resistance to life
250	NEUTRALITY	Emotions neither positive nor negative
200	COURAGE	Self-confidence and empowerment established
175	PRIDE	Influenced by external situations and people
150	ANGER	Hate/aggression and rage
125	GREED	Desire becomes insatiable
100	FEAR	Worry, anxiety or paranoia
75	GRIEF	Sadness or regret
50	DEPRESSION	Helplessness or Hopelessness
40	APATHY	Sense of resignation, emotionally empty
30	GUILT	Blame, blaming or being blamed
20	SHAME	Victimhood or humiliation

Expansion ↑ / Contraction ↓

As you can see from the emotional vibration chart, when you feel not good enough, you often carry guilt, shame or depression around, which are some of the lowest emotional vibrations. The implication of this is that you then attract lower vibrational events to you. Let us explore some of these emotions further.

Shame

As we can see, the chart shows shame has one of the lowest frequencies. It is also one of the most disruptive, destructive and deeply wounding feelings you can experience. When you are in shame, your self-worth is at an all-time low. The sense of unworthiness makes you bow your head and play small to life.

Holding shame is the cause of many a life challenge, especially debt, debilitating illnesses or making dysfunctional relationship choices. Shame goes much deeper than just feeling guilty. Often when you feel guilty, it is just a sense of regret or remorse over something you feel you should or shouldn't have done.

In shame, that guilt turns into an even deeper painful feeling inside you, and your negative mind chatter convinces you that you are a bad person, therefore there must be something wrong with you. You are likely to have a harsh inner judge, jury and jailer. Holding shame is one of the hidden causes of self-sabotage. Shame can create such a bleakness that sometimes you can feel you are so unredeemable that there is no way out.

Some examples of beliefs that shame may have stemmed from could be:

'I am unforgivable'.

'I am unworthy'.

'I am inadequate'.

'I am undeserving'.

'I am a bad person'.

'I am not good enough'.

'I am wrong'.

'I am flawed'.

'I have made such terrible mistakes'.

I distinctly remember the shame and humiliation a tyrannical teacher made me feel in school. Along with three other 'bad' pupils, we were forced to parade around the classroom showing all the other classmates our exercise books and revealing how messy our handwriting was. I can still feel the energy of that shame every time I remember the scenario.

Unfortunately, this action neither improved my handwriting nor made me feel good about myself. In fact, over the following years, it compounded and confirmed the belief so strongly that no matter what I did, it or I would never be perfect enough.

However, the continual feeling of shame can become a bit of an addiction, because at a very deep and probably unconscious level, you get to use it as a form of control. You get to control the people around you by playing the victim so they 'treat you bad', punish you, reject you or let you down. You attract relationships where you are continually saying sorry or apologising and often become so co-dependent and desperate to be loved, approved of or accepted that you will do anything to avoid the dreaded feeling of rejection.

When I was at my heaviest, I was in so much shame. The feeling was torturous and, unfortunately, my default action when experiencing such an intense emotion was to eat even more to quell and numb that feeling. Often, when around friends or clients, I could feel discord between us on the subject of my weight. This would then intensify my shame even more. To feel so out of control with an addiction lowers your self-esteem further and further down that emotional vibration scale. Every time I looked in the mirror, I couldn't bear what I saw, so out would come the beating stick and I would chastise myself further.

My partner was very polite about my weight and said he loved me for who I was, but, unfortunately, I could sense the hidden disapproval of my portion sizes, and this exacerbated my own self-disgust. I was always making excuses, such as pretending I needed the food for energy. Well, that's a lie, isn't it? How can you possibly have any energy if you are carrying an extra five stone around every day, especially in the job I had at the time, which involved doing a lot of physical work.

The next lie I would tell myself was, 'I have been at work all day, therefore I have a right to my hunger and to eat and fill myself up!' The truth is that I was suffering from so much inner shame that every effort I made to change was sabotaged by my own harsh inner critic. It was the typical vicious circle of shame; anxiety about the reactions of others = shame = more fear = disgust that I could not get my eating under control = shame = anger and rage at myself = eat = more shame for not sticking to my self-promise. I would feel an absolute failure yet again = more shame. More food. I was amazed at how my body kept going. The diet industry loved me! I bought every diet plan, tried diet shakes, went on weight-loss challenges, detoxed and even tried hypnosis. I constantly played weight-loss tapes and often went to sleep listening to 'How to achieve perfect weight loss' on various YouTube channels. I did achieve some success, but as soon as I seemed to be doing well and lost a stone, something would kick in that would sabotage me and the weight would pile back on, along with even more shame.

The only way change started was for me to look in the mirror and sincerely say, 'Wendy, I am so sorry. Please forgive me. Thank you. I love you just the way you are'.

Disheartenment

When you are suffering from I'mperfectionism, one of the common patterns is to keep comparing yourself to other people. Are they slimmer, prettier, with better biceps or six packs? Or it might be about comparing their intelligence, therefore making you feel incompetent or useless. What about the lifestyles and seeming success of others?

The challenge with comparing yourself to others is that very often you are trying to compare apples to oranges. It's as futile as telling an elephant he should be able to climb a tree and then because he can't (obviously!) and a monkey can, he gets told that he is useless. Of course you would start to feel disheartened.

Every time you judge yourself harshly as not good enough, or attack your self-esteem, you break a piece of your heart. No wonder you get disheartened. You have just 'dissed' your heart. On the emotional vibration chart, disheartenment is another one of those lower vibrations. The impact, then, is lack of success, poor health and troubled relationships.

Disheartenment also comes from consistently believing life MUST go your way. When you resist life and fight the realities you are faced with, you will undoubtedly lose. What if you could trust the process of life? How would that help you re-engage your heart? What if there were a loving Universe constantly guiding you to your dreams and potential? What if the seeming adversity, the different level of success or the physical body you have is perfect and right — for this moment? It doesn't mean you can't (or shouldn't?) change it, but taking the path of least resistance will help prevent you from getting disheartened along the way.

What could you do today to re-engage your heart at work, at home and with yourself? What judgement do you need to release?

Despair

After disheartenment can come despair. With disheartenment you feel as if the wind has been taken out of your sails, deflated like a balloon, or you just feel 'flat'.

With despair, there are significantly higher levels of panic, anxiety and possibly melancholy. The energy is exceptionally low and quite often all sense of hope diminishes. When you have the affliction of not feeling good enough most of the time, you can be convinced that nothing will ever change. This can further lead into a sense of depression.

> *When you have no hope, it can be difficult to cope.*
> —WENDYISM

Anger

Along with disheartenment and despair are very suppressed feelings of anger and frustration. However, the person not feeling good enough will likely believe they do not have the right to that anger or feel very scared to express it. They may be so shut down and disassociated that they are not even aware of how they feel. Often their experience of anger has been coloured many times by seeing it become a weapon used against people or presenting circumstances or their potential.

Would you agree that most feelings of not being good enough tend to stem from childhood? Whilst you accidentally took on that belief (because you didn't know any better at the time), when you look back to that time, you can often see how that belief may have created anger within you.

Maybe you got angry at your parents for comparing you with another sibling. Maybe you got angry because you were abandoned. Maybe you were angry because you could never prove or feel good enough for your parents, teachers or any other influential person.

The problem with anger is that it feeds on itself.

Have you ever started the day a bit grumpy?

On your way to work, you get stuck in a traffic jam and your frustration increases. At work, whilst carrying out your first job of the day — photocopying — the innocent photocopier breaks down! By now frustration has developed into annoyance and your co-workers start to piss you off. After leaving work, your normal route is closed, so you have a long diversion, making you miss an important appointment and, to add salt to the wound, you get charged for the appointment anyway. By the time you get home, you are so fraught you take it out on your partner, and you end up having a full-blown argument. On a scale of 1 (mild frustration) to 10 (full-blown fury), what started out as a 1 or 2 feeling is now at an intense 9 or 10. The anger has become completely displaced, disproportionate and destructive.

Now, if you imagine the consequence of the amplification of anger since childhood, you can start to see how many damaging patterns of behaviour may have sabotaged your success. The original hurt developed into frustration, which developed into anger, which developed into rage. Unhealed, it becomes one of the most devastating forces of nature! It wreaks havoc in relationships, creates disease/illness in the body and sends money and success into a downward spiral, to name just a few of its effects.

However, the feeling of anger is not, in itself, bad.

Clean anger acts like a boundary barometer. It allows you to feel that something is not right. Accordingly, clean anger lasts no more than about four seconds and is expressed in the tone of 'Pass the salt and pepper pot, please'. 'Your action of _____ triggers me to respond with anger'.

However, when you have stored, suppressed or unhealed anger, even just a little violation of your space can get met with an enormous reaction. Or you might have personally experienced a situation where something seemingly so trivial sparked off an almighty humdinger from your partner and you were probably left completely bewildered about what just happened.

I had a time when a very dear friend I was working with, Janet, started getting annoyed about something I was unintentionally doing. Unfortunately, she had never said anything to me about this in over two years of friendship, so I was completely oblivious to how she was feeling.

Then, one day, all that emotional buildup could be contained no longer, and she exploded at me! Naturally, I was left dazed and in shock, not to mention mortified that my actions had been causing her so much stress. Sadly, so big was the explosion between us that it completely ruined the trust and friendship we had. Perhaps it might have been avoidable if the annoyance/anger barometer had been employed much earlier. Maybe if I could have been much more conscious of the impact of my actions, I could have sensed something wrong earlier. At the same time, if she could have taken accountability of her feelings and reactions and said something much earlier, then we could have avoided our major falling-out.

We are seldom angry for the reason we think we are.

In metaphysics (the study of the Universal Laws), the Laws of Attraction and Reflection state that we are always unconsciously attracting, even inviting, energies/people/situations to us that are going to show us:

a) what we like about ourselves

b) what we hate about ourselves

c) where we are out of balance

d) what we believe about ourselves or others

e) how to help heal (see Chapter 2 for a more in-depth explanation)

For example:

Suppose you are carrying a belief you have held since childhood of not being good enough, and you are still feeling hurt and angry about that. It is likely you will unconsciously meet someone in the workplace who will undermine you, maybe keep interfering, micromanaging you or have some other irritating habit. How can you tell? You will feel annoyed, controlled, interfered with, not good enough, frustrated, unheard and, ultimately, you will probably want to quit!

Just remember though, wherever you go, there you are. They are not the cause of your anger; however, they may be the button pusher of your symptoms. Ultimately, on a spiritual level, they are there for your healing.

Nobody does to you what is not ultimately for you.
—WENDYISM

In my HEART therapeutic coaching (coaching that combines counselling), by working with these sorts of challenges and issues you are currently going through, we quickly get to the root causes of destructive emotions, beliefs and behaviours that are creating disharmony in your life. Obviously, you don't want to go around feeling angry, yet it's not about completely ridding the part of you that gets angry. If you 'cut off' that part altogether, you would never know how to discern, or be aware, when something is wrong, or when a boundary is being overstepped. Also, if you cut off anger completely, you cut off passion. It's the same physical energy.

Think about it for a moment.

Can a depressed person feel enthusiastic and passionate? No. When you suppress any emotion, you suppress its opposite too. If you don't acknowledge your sadness and grief, your joy cannot be truly expressed either. If you suppress your resentment and hatred, how can you feel love? If you ignore how insecure and anxious you are, how can you feel safe and trusting? If you smother your feeling of jealousy or envy, how will you feel gratitude and appreciation? All emotions are just energy — energy in motion, originating from a thought or belief.

Change the Thinking, Change the Feeling

Although we live in a dualistic world, the goal is to feel whole. Obviously, this doesn't mean going around acting angry, upset, jealous and the like, but by allowing yourself to feel the emotion, you can find the belief behind it. Now you can permit yourself to heal by dissolving the emotional energy that is no longer serving you. Naturally, you want to strive for peace, but being numb or suppressed is not peace. Peace comes from acknowledgement of what is and then rising to the highest emotional vibration you can in that moment. Ironically, you can feel peaceful with all your feelings. It is an acceptance that 'right now, right here, I am feeling angry, sad, fearful, and so on, and that's okay'. It is the resistance to the true feeling that causes problems.

Resentment

Resentment gets fuelled by the person not feeling perfect enough. They feel that no matter what they do for others, they never get the reward, the appreciation or the recognition. This can feel devastating to someone who already has low self-esteem. What started out genuinely as wanting to please, to be seen as the reliable, responsible one or the go-to person, crossed the line to resentment when their hidden agenda of doing things to avoid being disliked, rejected or not needed didn't prevent people from hurting them or letting them down. This really hurts the ego as well. A typical resentment expression is 'After all I have done for them …' The sacrificing martyr no longer enjoys what they are doing for others and now sees it as a burden, creating overwhelm and consequently feeling overstretched.

We have only just touched the tip of the iceberg of feelings associated with perfectionism and procrastination, and more will be covered in the coming chapters.

What do we do with all these feelings?

How to Overcome Blocked Emotions

One of the best tools I have come across is tapping. This is known by other names, such as emotional freedom tapping (EFT) or soul tapping.

The idea is to use the fingers to tap certain points of the body to tap and release the emotion and belief. The best way I can describe what EFT is would be to think about when a central-heating radiator gets an airlock in it and part of the radiator is cold because the heated water can't get round it. Usually tapping the radiator unblocks the airlock and the radiator gets hot again. So it is when your emotions have got stuck. It stops the energy flow. Tapping releases that block quickly. The best suggestion I can offer is to type EFT into a browser search bar and look at one of the many instructional diagrams.

Feelings Log

Another way is to write a feelings log. But in order to clear the feeling, explore what the belief is behind the emotion generated. Example:

Monday
Feeling: anger
Belief: Angry that I can't lose weight

Tuesday
Feeling: anxiety
Belief: Worried I am unable to pay my bills
… and so on

The Effects of Emotional Disharmony

Natalie was dealing with releasing addiction and came to see me because she felt very depressed. Her self-esteem was at an all-time low because she was feeling so much shame for 'using drugs and alcohol' to get through her day. Initially she wanted to 'blame' her husband because he was so unsupportive and also extremely demanding. She constantly felt alone and feared rejection if she said anything, so to compensate she desperately tried to keep herself, her children and her home immaculate.

Her desire to please quickly dissolved into resentment and she became more and more angry with her husband. Unfortunately, Natalie didn't feel she had a right to feel this anger, so she resorted to her coping skill of choice — drugs and alcohol — rather than facing the depths of her depression and hidden rage.

We set about looking where Natalie's feelings of unworthiness and not feeling good enough stemmed from, and the coping skills she adopted. We then proceeded to work on releasing her need for perfectionism to try to make people stay with her or treat her better. By increasing her own self-love and self-acceptance, her self-confidence immediately grew.

Now, she was able to take the pressure off herself to be perfect but, at the same time, learned to recognise her true perfection, and was able to make changes at home that allowed her to feel more secure within herself.

This gave Natalie the ability to make better decisions for herself and her family, because they were no longer based on the fear of rejection if she didn't 'toe the line'. Consequently, she was able to release the need to cope through drugs and alcohol and come from a new place of authenticity.

> *Your partner, parents or peers are not responsible for your happiness or tears, so be accountable to yourself right here and all of your own feelings and fears.*
> —WENDYISM

For your free bonus content go to www.imperfectasiam.today

CHAPTER 4

Failure, Fear and Other Flawed Feelings

When you make decisions through fear,
it will eventually cost you dear.
—WENDYISM

Whilst writing this book, I experienced a massive emotional roller coaster. When I first thought of the idea, it felt like the rush and headiness of a new relationship and I enthusiastically wrote several chapters, keen to make regular dates with my laptop and creative thoughts. And then, again, just like a new relationship, the uncertainty kicked in. I started finding fault with myself and what was wrong with the book. The self-doubt and self-attack soon caused my fragile self-confidence to come crashing down.

It was ironic, considering the title of this book, but I couldn't stop feeling that it wouldn't be good enough and that I wouldn't be respected for what I was saying. The thought of exposing myself to a worldwide market challenged my frail ego. Naturally, I wanted the book to do well, but the thought of doing a book tour looking the way I did filled me with the dread of ridicule and rejection. I had always lived a very natural life with my horses, but if I was going to be more successful in my business,

I would have to reveal my true self and, at that point in time, I did not feel good about myself at all.

I plunged deeper down into the depths of depression. Irrational fear paralysed every cell in my body and so prevented me from being able to do the very things that would help me move forward. This resulted in me 'procrastiweighting' (a Wendy word meaning 'the art of putting on the pounds whilst putting off the projects') for another two years about writing this book.

Consequently, even more debts and projects piled up, even more excuses and lies to myself piled in and even more weight piled on (yet another thirty pounds). My fears continued to deprive me of any confidence, disempowered me and drew me down to a complete halt. Would there be any way out? (Stay tuned to find out how I did overcome those fears.)

Nearly all our fears stem from a feeling of not being good enough, perfect enough or even just enough. When you lack confidence in yourself and your capabilities, fear can easily take over. Wondering if you look perfect enough or trying to appear to others as if you have a perfect life can set up an inner fear, which can lead to myriad coping strategies to alleviate or suppress hidden feelings of failure, of being flawed in some way.

Such is the fear of being unliked, unloved and uncared for. You become like a chameleon, changing your personality and your opinions in every situation to avoid that feeling of utter rejection.

Exercise: How Severe Is Your Fear?

Using the table below, indicate how intensely you feel each fear.

Fear	Not at all	A little	Somewhat	A lot	Off the scale
Rejection					
Abandonment					
Embarrassment					

Fear	Not at all	A little	Somewhat	A lot	Off the scale
Ridicule					
Being unlovable					
Failure					
Success					
Being shamed					
Competition					
Loss					
Being attacked					
Being harmed					
Confrontation					
Setting boundaries					
Being unliked					
Being unloved					
Being uncared for					
Losing control					
Change					
Intimacy					
'Getting it wrong'					
Making a mistake					
Commitment					
Being yourself					

When you are imprisoned by perfectionism or procrastination, you can be so paralysed with fear that you feel like a rabbit, frozen to the spot, in the headlights of a rapidly approaching vehicle. You know you must move — you know disaster is heading your way — BUT moving brings its own fear: the fear of making the wrong decision.

The Terror of Getting It Wrong

As a HEART Therapeutic Coach, one of the many groups of people I help is teenagers and their mums. A familiar pattern I see is parents or caregivers taking on the belief that they have failed when their kids seemingly go off the rails or exhibit upsetting behaviour (e.g. self-harming, panic attacks or depression, etc.).

This can often be a 'chicken and egg' situation. Did the sense of failure, for example, that the child acts out, stem from the mom or dad or did the sense of failure come from the child whom the parent feels guilty about? Who knows? Our energy is so intertwined. We can even pick up signals of our parents' emotional state when we are in the womb. It doesn't really matter; what is important is changing the belief. I especially believe parents must be willing to work on themselves if they really want to help their kids.

All too often troubled teenagers are referred to me, but the real source of the issue is the parental or family dynamic that the child is acting out. Parents don't often make enough time for themselves, let alone put some energy and time into their own personal development. In my experience, women are top of the charts from always sacrificing too much for their children.

My personal experience has been that the more the child is acting out, the more there are hidden (and sometimes not-so-hidden) emotions, beliefs and strategies going on in the parents' lives that the child is merely reflecting, taking on board or expressing because their parents are oblivious to the stuff that is contributing to the behaviour.

I am not saying parents are to blame, but I *am* saying parents need to be accountable for their beliefs and feelings.

One young girl I worked with, Libby, regularly dreaded going to school. Not from a normal child's rebellious 'I hate school' way, which we nearly all go through at some point growing up. No, school was terrifyingly traumatic for her EVERY single day. Each week that we worked together, I noticed Libby's anxiety getting worse, and her confidence was fast leaking out of her. Instead of finding a feeling of improvement, she would just sob uncontrollably on my shoulder every single time at the stress she felt. My heart would break every week, feeling like this was no way for a young girl to spend her youth.

One of the major pressures Libby felt was that she was just not good enough for her parents. She found learning in the physical school environment total torture, especially having to be around other students and teachers. She was convinced they were judging her, and this of course attracted bullying behaviour from them (and I include the teachers here).

Her parents both had extremely senior positions in the corporate world. From Libby's point of view, the pressure to perform and be the best in her class was enormous, especially since, unlike her parents, she was not a natural academic. It didn't help that her parents were just too busy to sit down with her and talk through her fears and frustration.

When I managed to eventually work with her father, I found that he was experiencing a lot of self-denial. Without realising it, the high-powered job he was in was also creating a feeling of immense pressure to perform. Secretly, because he was terrified of getting it wrong at work and putting his job at risk, he was leaking out his fears into the family environment. He, after all, could not admit to his feelings because then he would not only feel a failure at work, but also the sense of shame and of failing his family would 'tip him over the edge'.

Unfortunately, when we have these deep-rooted fears, someone is going to mirror them or act them out for you. This led to the father being angry and frustrated at his daughter all the time, which was merely reflecting his own anger and frustration at himself for not being perfect.

Meanwhile 'Mum', like most mums, was trying to be the peacemaker. Whilst caught up in the middle of feeling like she was failing Libby, failing her husband and failing to make it better, she didn't even have time to acknowledge her own terrifying thoughts of not being a good mother. If she sided with her husband, Libby felt betrayed or unheard, and if she supported her daughter, her husband would just get angry and controlling and their relationship would become strained. Trying to please her daughter, her husband, the rest of the family and her own boss, she just did not have the bandwidth to even please herself. No one was happy.

Thankfully, with the support of the horses and the HEART coaching, we managed to turn the family round by starting with the mother, helping her let go of the 'bad mother' belief and feeling a failure for not being the perfect parent, and getting her to find her truth and voice first. She stopped listening to the authorities and her husband's moaning, and instead listened to what SHE honestly wanted to do to support her daughter. The daughter finally felt heard, and a plan of action could be implemented.

Sadly, this situation is increasing in a lot of families and relationships. It is time to stop this cycle of self-destruction.

In my experience of coaching people to release perfectionism, I have found that one of the biggest worries behind not being good enough is the fear of rejection and of being disliked. Time and time again I see clients sacrificing their Truth and therefore sacrificing themselves and their real needs in a desperate attempt to be liked, loved or loveable.

'I am so sorry' started the frantic text at 10.30 p.m. 'I am so scared you will change your mind about me working with you' it went on to read. 'I am getting myself in such a state again, and I am feeling sick with anxiety because I have messed up ...'

In the pain of perfectionism, we can see fears come from low self-esteem and a sense of unworthiness. Usually, this stems from a time in the past when there was a sense of failure about something, getting told off or feeling something was your fault.

My business partner, Amazing Grace, had made a simple and easily done mix-up of a day and date in an email to clients attending a forthcoming workshop. It hadn't had any major consequences and, because of her normal efficiency, I had been copied in on the correspondence to the clients and so I just happened to notice this — almost by accident. I instantly sent an extra email clarifying the correct day and date to the clients with a little joke in it. No big deal to me, but for Amazing Grace, well, she felt she had committed the cardinal sin of Making a Mistake! She had got something wrong; it wasn't perfect. Unfortunately for Amazing Grace, such was her fear of someone finding fault that she kept drawing that experience to herself. Unfortunately, there had been a particular traumatic event when one perfectionist boss she worked for humiliated her by having her escorted off the premises for a similar small failing.

Naturally, after such a traumatic experience, her fear got heightened, her confidence got lowered and her body got sicker through the stress to 'get it right'.

In a reassuring reply to her text, I explained I wanted a human being working with me, not a robot. It was a simple slip. Amazing Grace's normally high standard of excellence was not in question for one moment to me, but for Amazing Grace her fear was that the lack of everything being 100 percent perfect was going to bring her whole world crashing down. Such is the plague of perfectionism.

> *When you live with the fear of rejection,*
> *You are held hostage by those in your situation.*
> —WENDYISM

Out of all the myriad fears, especially those around things not being perfect or good enough, the fear of rejection comes in at number one. Such is the desperate need to be loved, approved of or accepted by others that we go to great lengths to create masks, illusions or impressions of being perfect. Why?

When did we learn that being ourselves was not good enough? The truth is revealed in Chapter 6.

The reality is that you are good enough just the way YOU are, and when YOU stop rejecting you and love yourself as YOU, you will find you have the antidote to the fear of rejection.

Fiona's Fear of Rejection from a Friend

It was 10.30 p.m. when Fiona received a distressed text from a friend and work colleague. Her friend desperately needed some advice for an especially important pitch she had to give that week to a big corporate organisation. There were a few exchanges of communication, and it transpired that it wasn't just an odd bit of feedback and help her friend wanted, but a whole strategy for this corporate company she was bidding for work with.

Fiona noticed that after receiving a request for something so much more in-depth and so late at night, she got a gut feeling of being 'taken' from. Naturally with friends we would want to help here and there for free, but on this occasion, Fiona felt that a boundary had been crossed.

Fiona felt in a predicament. She wanted to support her friend but didn't feel good about giving an hour's consultancy call for free, especially as that was her livelihood. However, there was a feeling of risk about asking for money because it might damage their friendship. Most of us hate the thought of rejection, and Fiona was no exception; having to change a lifetime pattern of doing things for free — in order to feel valued or accepted by others — was a huge deal for her.

Fiona sent a reply to her friend stating that, as this was more of a consultancy-type call, she would have to charge, and she trusted that her friend would understand that this was a 'business thing' and not about their friendship.

Fiona's friend immediately sent her a reply stating that she herself wasn't getting paid directly for the pitch and that MAYBE if all went well when she pitched to the company, and IF she managed to get work with them, THEN, possibly, she would be in a position to hire Fiona.

At this point, Fiona recognised her friend's 'carrot-dangling' pattern and, as she reflected over their friendship and working arrangement, she realised her friend was constantly dangling carrots in front of her, getting her to work for free because it MIGHT lead to getting hired at some point in the future. In two years, Fiona hadn't received any work from her friend. Despite many hours of free consulting and support, NOTHING had ever come back to her.

Fiona courageously replied that she totally understood, but on this occasion, she was going to have to decline taking the call for free and wished her friend well with the project. As she put the phone down, far from feeling rejected, Fiona felt formidable. She was delighted with herself for having had the courage to set clear financial boundaries with her friend, and because she had properly valued herself, the self-worth feeling she had was just as great as if she had received payment anyway.

Fiona was jubilant at breaking a lifetime pattern.

'I now STOP allowing people to make me believe that I am the one in so much need that it's okay for them to walk all over me. No more!' she fearlessly declared.

Fear of Confrontation

The less you value yourself, the more the need to keep everyone else onside becomes important to you. This can often mean not having the courage to speak up or speak your Truth because of the fear of confrontation, which may lead to rejection.

'What if they get upset?' I hear you worriedly ask.

Let me ask you this question instead: 'Why is it okay that the other person is NOT allowed to get upset but YOU are, and why is it NOT okay to let them know how you honestly feel?'

Can you see how detrimental that is to your self-worth and self-esteem? The problem is that if you continue 'doing things' for a quiet life or biting your tongue rather than saying what you feel or think, there will come a point when that suppression manifests itself in some way.

There will either be a great out-and-out argument, which may come out subtly in the form of a disease or an illness, or it could manifest itself by adversely affecting your finances. Maybe the conflict you have with the person you feel you can't talk to will come out in a displaced way to someone who has nothing to do with the problem.

The boss shouts at the husband, who goes home and shouts at his partner, who shouts at the kids, who shout at the dog, and so on.

I appreciate that there are certain times that are not ideal for confrontations, and certain people who are not safe to confront (or, indeed, are not worth confronting).

Years ago, when I was with a violent alcoholic partner, he came home in a foul mood after yet another binge-drinking bout. This was not the time for me to stand up to him and try to get my needs met or say how I felt. However, one day, when he was calm and sober and we were in a public place, I knew the time was right for me to find the courage to start expressing my feelings and fears to him.

As nothing ultimately changed, I then had to find more courage to create a self-loving strategy to release myself from that situation altogether. Having said this, I am aware that anyone who has been in a similar situation knows that although you are too scared to stay, paradoxically, you are also too scared to leave.

The secret is to value yourself enough to speak your Truth as soon as someone (or something that has happened) upsets you. The challenge is to move through the fear that if you stand up for yourself, you will upset them and then they will reject you.

Remember, you do not have the power to upset someone, nor they you. It is all about making the choice of how to react.

> *If, in a relationship, you cannot be you,*
> *then what you have is not completely true.*
> —WENDYISM

Fear of Failure/Success

Another two of the great enablers of procrastination and perfectionism are the fears of success and failure. What I have observed from working with my clients is that success and failure fears are just opposite ends of the same fear.

Quite often the presenting fear of completing a project may seem to be the fear of it not being good enough, but what if the fear is that it IS good enough? What then?

Most people are already 'doing' failure. When you say, 'Oh, it might not work — it's too much of a risk', you think you are expressing your fear of failure. Is not the fear of doing what you really want exactly that — failing?

Or is it really a cop-out?

What if it goes great?

What if it is a success? What then?

Could the real fear be that of being judged?

If it does go well, are you afraid that you won't be liked by your circle of friends because you have broken the code of failure? Often, in a circle of underperforming friends or family, when someone steps up, unconsciously it challenges other people to feel they must make changes, or it highlights their own lack of success. These types of people usually criticise your efforts or sabotage your success.

The idea of success could bring about the belief that there will be even more work, responsibility, pressure, demands on your time and energy, and so on. When you are already feeling knackered from procrastination (it takes a lot of energy to not do something), the thought of success can be exhausting and overwhelming.

Yet another possibility could be that you will have to change your story. If you played the 'procrastinating failure card' most of your life, succeeding could mean that you have a completely new identity to find.

One of my clients, who was struggling to let go of her old identity, would often call me. She was concerned because she felt as if she were dying. I reassured her that when we let go of old patterns and inner personality traits, it can feel like a death of sorts. But we are just dying to the old as we make way for the new, exactly the way the caterpillar breaks free from the cocoon and transforms into a beautiful butterfly.

Reassuringly though, when you do start to love and accept yourself just the way you are, fears of 'success' or 'failure' will not have power over you anymore. This is because you no longer need the validation of success to make you feel good enough. You are able to value yourself, whatever you achieve or don't achieve.

Loss of Confidence

Not feeling good enough is one of the biggest causes of confidence loss. When you have lost confidence in yourself and your abilities, all your other fears get amplified: fear of rejection, not getting it right, confrontation, failing and even fear of succeeding! After all, if you are not feeling confident, then your fear creates further worries about how you are going to handle all the extra responsibility, demands from people, increased income, and other trappings of success.

How can you be brimming with confidence one minute and then feel so utterly anxious the next? Where does confidence go? In truth, it doesn't go anywhere. It is still there. The problem is that it has been buried under false beliefs, unhelpful behaviours, blocked emotions and a host of other stories, scripts and stresses.

Once you uncover what is really behind the loss of confidence, you can start to change the belief or behaviour and break free from your anxious and limiting self-talk.

When you are out of balance, according to the Laws of Attraction and Reflection, you will naturally draw to you someone who is going to either mirror and reflect the parts of you that need integrating or help you rebalance in some way.

How to Dissolve the Fear — The 'So What' Principle

I tend to use the 'So what' principle to send a defiant energy to the fear, especially when it involves people.

For example, I had a young client experiencing a high level of social anxiety. I taught her to keep saying 'so what' to her fears like 'My friends might not like me'.

'So, what if they don't, then what?'

'Well, I would be on my own'.

'So, what if you are, then what?'

'Well, I'd be lonely'.

'So, what then? What would you do?'

'I would cry'.

'And so, what if you cried, what then?'

'I guess I would eventually stop'.

'Yes, and so what would you do then?'

'Talk to some different people'.

'So now how does that feel?'

'Much better'.

Now try the exercise on one of your fears.

In the coming chapters, we will explore further ways to dissolve the fears and anxieties that plague the perfectionist and procrastinator.

Thankfully, I always believe life happens 'for us' rather than 'to us', so when recent life events on a global scale forced us all to slow down and face ourselves, I, too, had the courage to look at my fears, flaws and failings and dispel their lies.

Then a miracle happened. During the COVID lockdown, my publisher ran a free 7-Day Book-Writing Challenge, and it was just the kick up the proverbial that I needed. I finally faced both the tyrant of terror within me and the relationship with my 'book lover' not being good enough. I recommitted to my writing and eventually finished my book. Ironically, as I faced my fears each day, my confidence grew higher and higher, and my old 'Wendy Woo' spark ignited again.

For your free bonus content go to www.imperfectasiam.today

CHAPTER 5

Change the Self Script

*How you communicate to you
attracts how others will do too.*

— WENDYISM

What if you could …

Stop beating up on yourself and believe you are good enough?

Stop feeling anxious or angry or acting aggressively towards yourself or others because that project had a mistake in it?

Trust the process of being imperfectly perfect?

Finally be set free from your self-imposed prison of perfectionism or procrastination?

Envision a world of self-kindness, self-care and self-confidence for you?

What would the wonderful improvements to your life be, and how would you benefit?

A few years ago, when I was personally imprisoned by my own procrastination, it felt as though my whole 'internal workforce' went on strike. The complicated thought processes my relentless mind chatter went through were horrendous. The viciousness of my inner voice would have had me locked up for real if I had dared to speak to someone like that in my outer world.

My 'internal ruthless employer' constantly hissed at my 'internal staff' about how useless they were and what complete and utter failures they were. They became totally fed up with being told they weren't good enough.

The emotional pain I was in at that time was so intense that it started to reflect physically in many parts of my body. Many a time I just wanted to stay in bed in my darkened room. Angry with the world, angry with my 'internal staff' being on strike, angry at my 'internal boss' for being so harsh, angry with myself for making so many mistakes in my life, angry at life being such a struggle, angry at the past, angry that I couldn't get 'the oomph' to change things, angry at others for having what I wanted, angry that I had invested thousands of pounds on courses, workshops and online stuff, yet my business was still not thriving nor was I feeling good enough. I was angry, angry, angry. But I could not, dared not, show this rage to the world. Instead, somehow, I managed to drag myself to my feet each day, stuff my feelings back down, put on my 'happy face' and tackle another day.

I was particularly good at hiding my depression; after all, I had spent a lifetime hiding my feelings of hurt and confusion experienced in childhood, but that pain and anguish took its toll on my physical body, and no amount of diets I went on could shift the weight of emotions tightly stuck in every excess pound I carried. Thank God for my horses and clients needing me. They literally saved my life. At least I had a reason to get up every day.

Ironically, once I was 'away from my manic mind' — having to think of others and help them — my inner distress quickly shifted. But as soon as I was 'back with me', the torture resumed, the inner bullying voice got louder and the fear of not getting things perfect enough resulted in me staying paralysed in my procrastination. The internal judge, jury and jailer kept extending my prison sentence with no chance of parole.

When you are seeking perfection from yourself or others, the energy that comes from you is very demanding. The resulting feeling in you AND them is that of being diminished, discouraged and demoralised. The part of you that is always doing its best will feel deflated from its efforts when you launch into yet another barrage of self-attack. The staff member that gave their all will feel bad, and then they start to believe they can only do wrong in your eyes. This energy separates rather than connects. It causes resentment, resistance and reluctance to want to do a good job. Even if you are not an employer, your inner 'staff' will be feeling the same response. This is one of the key causes of procrastination, which is the opposite of perfectionism.

Releasing Sacrifice

One of the symptoms many I'mperfectionists have of 'not feeling good enough' is always 'going into sacrifice'. They give up on their own needs regularly because they are so desperate to be loved, approved of or accepted. The fear of rejection if things, or they themselves, aren't perfect is often off the scale. They give and give and over-give, believing that this will be all it takes to get other people to recognise their worth.

But sacrifice is not true giving! It has a huge price on it. On the surface, it looks magnanimous that someone is being so selfless, thinking of other people all the time. However, it's not really coming from a self-less truth. In fact, in a lot of cases, it's a hidden lie. 'I only want to give to you providing that you don't abandon me', or 'Please like me and I will do anything for you', or 'If I give to you, I get to be superior'.

How can you tell if it's sacrifice?

It is as if your 'sacrifice sub-personality' has an internal tally sheet of what you have given out and what others have given back to you. On an unconscious energy exchange level, that part of you would know if they are in credit or whether they owe you, which, if this is the case, will probably leave you feeling resentful. Worse still, if the person doesn't meet your secret bargaining need by staying with you, loving you or approving of you, you are likely to feel betrayed, angry or hurt.

This is often further exacerbated because, under the Laws of Attraction and Reflection (Chapter 2), I can guarantee you have somebody selfish in your life who is frustrating the hell out of you. Remember, to the degree you are out of balance on one side of the pendulum, you will attract someone equally out of balance on the other.

The other way to tell if it's sacrifice is 'playing the martyr'.

'I have to do all this, but I don't get any reward, recognition or appreciation, so aren't I hard done by?'

'After all I did for them, they treat me like this'.

Martyrs have the PhD in victimhood and are always roping everyone into their drama, constantly trying to get sympathy and pity for their plight but not willing to do anything about the situation to change it. They secretly thrive on the drama and playing the victim.

The thing is, if you don't allow yourself to receive as well, you end up giving from an empty tank. What people get is your dregs, your exhaustion and your hidden resentment. That's why learning to be selfish is extremely important to the person who seemingly gives, gives, gives.

Expressing Your True Voice

Unfortunately, if you have learned to grow up as a martyr or live in sacrifice, it usually stems from losing the confidence to express yourself honestly for fear of making a mistake, upsetting someone or being rejected. When you were growing up, did you ever believe 'children should be seen and not heard'?

When did you lose the courage to speak up?

What was (and is now) the fear of expressing your truth?

A typical perfectionist pattern is to retreat into your shell when you're feeling not good enough. You are likely to go along with everything just for a quiet life. Because there is usually truly little confidence and even less self-esteem, it is extremely easy to not speak up, or say yes when you mean no. You fear rejection, so you are unlikely to set boundaries for fear of being disliked.

Not speaking up at all or hiding your truth is both bullying to yourself and passive-aggressive bullying to others, which ultimately encourages other people to intimidate you. This does not bode well for your soul, as the word *bullying* is spelled bul-LYING. Every time you go against your truth, a piece of your heart breaks because you are lying and a part of you will feel betrayed and belittled.

Finding the Courage to Express Your Voice and Real Choice

Think about a situation where you have not been able to speak your truth and find the belief you were running, maybe: 'If I say what I mean, they might reject me'.

How does that belief make you feel?

Now feel into that emotion.

'If I were to guess how old I was when I first felt this, I was probably at the age of _____.' Trust your first answer.

What was it about that situation that made you decide it wasn't safe to express your truth?

When I was about ten years of age, I remember going to a birthday party for one of my school friends. She was being annoying and a bit of a madam to everyone, and so when her mother asked me how I was enjoying the party I expressed honestly how I felt about my friend and her demeaning behaviour. I distinctly remember the reaction from her mother and her retort, 'Oh, well, we had better not invite you again, then'.

From that moment, I took on the belief that it's not safe to tell the truth. Consequently, I've had a lifetime of not speaking my truth because of my fear of rejection. However, having finally grown in self-esteem, I realise that holding back my truth has backfired so many times that I might just as well be honest to start with and save time, because not coming from the truth ultimately doesn't save friendships. Unfortunately, such is the need for safety, love and approval that the young inner child would unlikely be able to get that awareness to stay true.

> *When you make it true for you, you make it true for them.*
> —WENDYISM

It doesn't mean there won't be a few boats rocked, or that everyone will like what you say, but the reason this is such a powerful principle is that it will change the quality of people in your life. If you have been secretly (bul)lying (to) yourself and the world, who is that going to attract? Yes, people (bul)lying (to) you and not coming from their complete truth either.

Conversely, if you become wholly truthful to yourself and those around you, that principle now draws far more honest people to you. It CANNOT be any other way with the Laws of Attraction and Reflection.

> *Say what you mean, mean what you say,*
> *and then everyone can have a good day!*
> —WENDYISM

The by-product of this principle is that, because you're coming from your truth, you can set good boundaries. This is a high self-esteem action. When you are in this self-loving state, there is no fear of rejection, therefore no fear of 'getting it wrong', and so you can now relax and let go of everything having to be unnaturally perfect. Don't worry that your standards might slip, because now you have such positive high regard for yourself that you will naturally want to create excellence. But remember from Chapter 1, perfectionism and excellence are two completely different things.

The Power of Self-Love

Honest self-love (as opposed to self-aggrandisement) is one of the most powerful forces in the world. Not only does self-love give you courage, confidence, and conviction but additionally, when you are 'vibrating at the love frequency', you attract miracles, your life flows more easily and the world around you is benefitting from your loving light. Manifestations are easier and the Law of Attraction seems to work now (it always did, but your lower vibration would have kept away your desires).

The self-love symptoms:

- You don't put up with people's poor behaviour.
- You are healthily selfish.
- You speak your truth.
- You are kind to yourself.
- You accept failures, imperfections and mistakes as part of life, and don't beat yourself up for getting it wrong.
- You don't make yourself wrong.
- You choose for yourself first, knowing that only when your tank is filled are you then able to truly give to others.
- You love and accept yourself exactly as you are.
- You say 'I'mperfect as I am!'

… Something had to change from that unkind, unfair and unloving cell I was imprisoned in. I finally found the key to release myself from this life sentence of hard labour. The key? To love myself unconditionally found me a freedom I didn't know existed. It wasn't easy in the beginning, because a lifetime of self-attack was a difficult pattern to break. However, as I began realising it was safe to love myself and speak my truth, my 'internal staff' soon became willing to come back to work. I found a renewed enthusiasm for my projects. My deep depression lifted as I found the courage to feel my feelings, which resulted in me being empowered, energised and excited to be alive again. The more I increased my self-love, the more my life restarted and even my finances came back into the flow. I gradually realised I was good enough as I was, everything doesn't have to be 100 percent perfect and, whilst some people did leave my life, I could see that the kind of people I was now attracting were genuine and more honest.

How to Rewrite Your Childhood Scripts

The most amazing part of living as a human being is, even when life is feeling difficult, you are never fully stuck. As an 'infinite creator', you have been given a powerful gift — the ability to completely rewrite your story. No matter how 'prodigal-son-like' you have been (meaning no matter how much you have messed up), the moment you turn back to truth and let go of your stories is the moment your whole life will change.

If you have been telling yourself for years 'You are not worthy', 'You are not good enough' or 'You have to be perfect to be loveable' and other self-diminishing scripts, it's no wonder that your life seems to suck at times, your success gets sabotaged or you just about exist in a half-life.

Now it's time to change all that.

> *If you are not happy, nobody else needs to change, just you.*
> —WENDYISM

Change what you are putting out there about yourself and your life.

Exercise: Changing the Script

Before you can change the scripts, you need to discover when they started, where they came from and why they are there. Ask yourself, 'Of all the stories I am telling about myself, why do I want to keep repeating this same story that I am not good enough?'

Write down your answers, followed by: 'If I were to guess when I first told myself I was not good enough, it was probably at the age of _____.'

'If I were to guess what was happening, it was probably something to do with _____.'

'If I were to guess what was the real need not being met, it was probably _____.'

'How can I meet/give myself that need now, in the present?'

'What is the fear of loving myself?'

'What is the fear of how other people might react to me?'

'Why am I afraid of my life changing?'

There may be some other fears or concerns wanting to surface, so take a moment to connect with yourself and keep asking: 'Is there anything else that could be stopping me from wanting to love myself completely — just the way I am?'

Next, change those beliefs to a more positive affirmation of yourself.

'I love and accept myself just the way I am'.

'I am loved, loving and loveable just as I am'.

'I now love and approve of myself just the way I am'.

'I'm perfect just the way I am'.

However, if you find you are arguing with yourself as you say these affirmations, for example, if you say 'I love and accept myself' but hear 'No, you don't', then another way you can change your story is to talk to your Higher Self and ask, 'Show me how I can love and accept myself just the way I am', or 'Show me how I am loved, loving and loveable'.

This shift in focus helps to silence the argumentative part of your mind. Rather than saying what feels like a lie at that moment, you are asking 'how to', which can't be argued with. This tip is very helpful when you struggle to change what you are feeling about yourself. Because your Higher Mind has been set a challenge, it will now bring you all the ways you can be loved, loving and loveable. One caveat on this: sometimes when you have sent out an intention like this, the Universe can show you the opposite first. In other words, the blocks to allowing yourself to be loved, loving and loveable. This is where trusting the process is important.

To help minimise this, choose to consciously work on bringing up the reasons that you don't believe you can be loved, loving and loveable. Anything that needs changing in your life is down to the changing of your belief system.

The most important part of the exercise is giving to yourself now what you believe you didn't get back then.

Why is that important?

Because if you spend your whole life wanting the outside world to fix your inside dilemmas and dissatisfaction, you are going to be a long time looking. (Let me save you fifty years of researching that premise!)

It is all very well having a tantrum that Mum/Dad/teacher/friend/sibling/whoever didn't do it right or didn't love you the way you decided they should have, but the reality is that they did it the way they thought best, rightly or wrongly. The truth is that if you are still being affected by the past actions of others in your present life, it is pretty likely that you are doing the same as them right now, maybe not to others but almost certainly to yourself. It might be in a different form, but what you think you didn't get is what you are not giving to yourself right now.

What if you really could change your childhood script now?

You could finally be set free from your self-imposed prison of perfectionism or procrastination.

Surely speaking to yourself with more self-kindness, self-care and self-confidence is the more compassionate way to live now.

> *Your outside world can't change*
> *before your inside world has.*
> —WENDYISM

For your free bonus content go to www.imperfectasiam.today

CHAPTER 6

Rooting Out the Causes

No number of pills, potions or people can heal on the outside what can only be healed from the inside and Source!

—WENDYISM

In previous chapters, we have explored the principle, what you sow is what you grow, the Spiritual Law of Cause and Effect, and that everything you experience in life originates with a thought. Remember that those thoughts then become a belief. Beliefs create an experience, even if you are not conscious of it. That experience now creates another belief (or an assumption). These beliefs then create yet another experience, which you react to, and then that experience creates another belief, assumption or even a vow. And so the cycle continues. Beliefs get more entrenched, assumptions are presumed more often and vows are more regularly declared. It's time to discover not only the root causes of your beliefs, behaviours and blocked emotions, but how to move through them, change your inner scripting and subsequently upgrade your life.

A child's (let's call him 'Billy') radar senses these feelings of resentment and overwhelm. There is no way of knowing that the feeling Billy is picking up isn't about him. Probably his parents are unaware they are sending out this resentful energy; they are just feeling tired, exasperated and overextended. Billy innocently makes demands to be taken care of and then senses that his parents are getting more irritable and consciously —or unconsciously—they blame Billy for the reason they are feeling so swamped.

At this point, Billy is feeling confused; his parents are saying they love him on one hand, but on the other, the feelings he is picking up aren't congruent. Again, Billy takes on the belief that he must be at fault with the resulting thought: 'Next time I had better be quieter, less demanding!'

Billy's worry increases as that feeling of love diminishes. His new strategy is to not make demands and to hide his needs. By the time he has reached adulthood, Billy has been so used to sacrificing his real needs he is probably now acting as a doormat. He could even develop obsessional behaviours to be absolutely perfect in all he does, and the thought of getting anything even remotely wrong or of bothering people is terrifying and often creates so much anxiety, he avoids taking risks and starts to procrastinate and stay in unhealthy toxic situations.

When events happen around you and to you, especially in your formative years, it's very easy to make guesses or assumptions that this event (or someone's actions) means x y z. Accordingly, you then adopt coping strategies and behaviours that create a story to make sense to yourself of what is going on.

Conversely, Billy may feel so angry at not having his needs met that he rebels and demands that everyone meet his needs. He becomes the perfectionist boss, the demoralising partner, the tyrannical parent. No mistakes are allowed to be made, he finds fault in everything and everyone and anything less than perfect is totally unacceptable. The trouble with this strategy is that no one gets to feel good, his work colleagues feel disheartened, his partner walks on eggshells, terrified of upsetting him, and his children will likely feel so anxious that they find school terrifying because they fear they will not be able to meet his unrealistic expectations. Nobody is experiencing joy, freedom or confidence. Just discouragement, resentment or apprehension.

As a child, you are like a sponge, absorbing all the energies around you. Even in the womb, you are picking up what is going on with your mum, the environment and the thoughts and feelings around you collectively. Once you are born, it's as if you have a type of radar, and you use this constantly to work out what you need to do to safely get through life. Your primary motivation is to ensure you don't get abandoned, so you explore the best strategies, behaviours and coping skills you can come up with to manipulate everyone around you to achieve this goal.

However, in your innocence of understanding what is really going on, you frequently put two and two together and come up with seven. Here are some possible scenarios and the impact that they could have on your thinking.

'Mum and Dad split up. It must be my fault. I must have done something wrong'. Enter the strategy 'I must always get it right from now on'. The feeling that you must have done something wrong stays with you, so the assumption is that if you get something wrong or it is your fault, you will be rejected and abandoned. This is how the pattern of perfectionism can start.

Another example: One or both parents are having a really hard time with responsibility. They don't know how to balance work, rest and play, or how to give themselves some 'me time'. They are feeling overwhelmed, frustrated and probably resentful about everything they are trying to cope with.

Titania was the epitome of the above. She had been on both sides of the pendulum. After her parents had gone through a messy divorce, her father was so caught up in his wife's betrayal that he kept taking that anger out on Titania. She could never do anything right and her feelings were constantly dismissed. If she got upset, she was told to pull herself together and be strong. Consequently, she grew up believing her feelings didn't count and she wasn't important enough. To Titania, this meant she wasn't good enough. This saw her swing from the depths of depression to releasing her emotions hysterically. Her relationships with people were volatile, and she was often misunderstood and dismissed. No matter how perfect she tried to be in her work, no one seemed to validate her. She was always overlooked in promotions and if she ever tried to voice the unfairness, she was told to stop being a troublemaker. The feelings of inadequacy and not being good enough overwhelmed her.

Resentment, Revenge, Retaliation

To prove what a messed-up job your parents did, you either set out to prove their 'wrongness' by trying to be perfect or retaliate and go off the rails to really show them how they messed up. You blame them for failing to give you what *you* thought you wanted or needed.

Unfortunately, blaming them (or anyone else, for that matter) for why your life is not working, or you are the way you are, is just a major cop-out. That resentment is such a huge waste of energy.

Blame produces guilt; guilt produces punishment.

You will either be the punisher or the punished. There is no way out.

Accountability does not blame.

Accountability is different. It accepts a level of responsibility but sees the bigger picture. True accountability is not about blame, blaming or being blamed. It's holding one's hands up, taking responsibility and then seeking a way to change the situation.

In higher-consciousness thinking, accountability is an innocence or recognition of ignorance of information. It is easy to see how everyone is, or was, doing the best they can and yes, there is a way of doing things differently, with hindsight and new awareness.

Whilst it may seem unfair initially, the way to change these patterns from the past is to accept that, at some level, *you chose* to think that it was your fault. *You chose* to believe you weren't good enough. I can almost hear some of you saying, 'Yes, but I was only a child, how can it be *my* fault? I didn't know any different', and you are absolutely right — on one level.

However, as with anything or anyone you are blaming, if it is 'their' fault, or if you are just at the mercy of life's cruel joke, then you remain a victim; powerless and unable to change anything. Rather than demanding that the outside world changes, change must come from the inner world within you.

But what if you could be willing to see that in those past moments you chose to believe—rightly or wrongly—that you weren't good enough? What if you could be willing to see how you chose—again, rightly or wrongly—to vow to be perfect? Can you see that the moment that you make it your choice, this allows you to be accountable (not blaming yourself, though)? From here you are now able to make changes because you are the ONLY one in charge of your life. You are now back in control and empowered.

After expressing her initial rage about the principle of choice and accountability, Titania was willing to explore that. With some powerful coaching questions (we were also combining the coaching with the horses that day for extra insight), Titania was able to go back to times in her childhood and change those beliefs. She looked at the needs she didn't get met at the time and explored how she could give *herself* what she needed now. Titania was also able to go deeper and see what was really happening with her father, which resulted in her developing a whole new level of compassion and forgiveness for him. Her self-esteem grew enormously, and her attitude to her bosses changed. Interestingly, when she went back to work, she was offered the job role she was seeking.

This victim energy is probably one of the biggest sources of not feeling 'good enoughness'.

How to Release Trauma and Traumatic Events

Trauma, or traumatic events, come high on the list of causes of perfectionism, procrastination and other feelings of not being good enough. Many of my clients have been through various forms of abuse, and it's no wonder that they have taken on strategies to cope with those deep feelings. Understandably, blame may be part of the process, but when something quite traumatic happens, I believe it's even harder to shake.

It's as though the trauma permeates every cell of your body (which, in a way, the memory and emotion do) and this feeling of being out of control with that event is usually what sparks the downwards spiral.

Often, these feelings of shame, suppressed rage, depression and bewilderment plague someone who has sustained trauma. This individual will spend a lifetime trying to prove that they are perfect enough, but at the very core of their being, they have that inner voice taunting them, 'Of course you are not good enough'. They go through life feeling totally unsafe, and they believe the only way through it is to be perfect. Their self-esteem is so low it's practically nonexistent.

Or they may go into forms of self-harming because they are blaming themselves so much. Many self-harmers can only find relief from their emotional pain when they are either in physical pain or making themselves feel bad. Life becomes more and more dysfunctional with so many unhealthy, unsuitable and unavailable people around them. The only real antidote is learning how to love themselves.

So, What Exactly Is Self-Love?

What does it look like?

How do we know we are being loving to ourselves?

The answer is quite simple. Is how you are treating yourself the way you would treat your best friend?

Ninety percent of the time, the answer is no. Somewhere along the way, usually during childhood, you decided it's okay to be unkind to yourself, to constantly criticise and attack yourself for every minute misdemeanour and then punish yourself mercilessly for not getting it right. The irony is (on an unconscious level) that there is a part of you that thinks this IS the most loving thing you can do for yourself in that moment, albeit a very misguided strategy. However, you need to sit that part of you down and invite it to find a new way to love you.

Today Is Your Past

All behaviours, beliefs, assumptions and vows you have had in the past are like seeds sown that naturally will harvest a crop of experiences (remember the Law of Cause and Effect). When you start sowing new seeds of self-loving beliefs and adopt new behaviours, you can sometimes get discouraged by your crops not coming to fruition quick enough. In fact, because there are so many seeds sown—that is, old beliefs that you were unaware of still coming to fruition—it's easy to think that your new seeds aren't growing and therefore your new beliefs and strategies are not working.

Just notice that those experiences are still popping up, and reaffirm that you love yourself fully now, and thank them, but you no longer need those outdated coping skills. It becomes like a new muscle being worked. Keep repeating positive self-talk every day, and soon self-love will flow through with ease. When you are fully comfortable with loving yourself, you'll find that you will be quick to defend your newfound strategies.

What is always rewarding to hear from my clients is that as soon as they became better at self-love, they really did see a difference in the type of people they were attracting in their lives. Some of them had to make decisions to let go of certain people who didn't treat them with respect or kindness. Whilst for some it may be difficult rejecting people (and sometimes family), ultimately, the truth is that if other people can't love you for you, they are not worth your time and effort.

As the L'Oréal advertisement states, 'Because you're worth it!' Yes, you ARE worth it! The changes in your life become truly miraculous when you really believe this.

The Illusion of Normality

It's often an accepted fact that the highest percentage of abuse and trauma happens to women; however, I have personally had an increasing number of male clients come forward and find the courage to share their shame, embarrassment and confusion about such events.

Jerry was such a young man. Outwardly, to look at him, he looked 'normal' and successful. Nothing in his demeanour or his day-to-day life would indicate otherwise. However, when we started working together, the toll of keeping up this facade every day was eroding his self-esteem, his self-confidence and self-love. His coping skill that came from a traumatic period in his life was to make sure he always did everything perfectly and to always follow the rules. He was desperate to be liked and often sacrificed his truth to make sure everyone around him was happy. His fear of rejection was off the scale.

When he came to see me, he was due to present some important information to the directors of a big company. For most people, public speaking fills them with dread, and Jerry was no exception. Even though the group of men he was presenting to was small, the fear of being judged or getting it wrong was so overwhelming that he felt sick with anxiety and every part of his being wanted to run away.

In nature when a prey animal narrowly escapes being killed or when they feel threatened, their instinct is to run and flee the situation as quickly as possible. If they are unable to take flight, they will fight, and if they can't fight, they will freeze and often play dead. As soon as the threat is over, they will continue to run anyway. This helps to release the chemical effect of that trauma from their body and allows them to continue with their day.

We humans also feel equally threatened by the 'predators' of bosses, directors or other colleagues and therefore naturally want to experience that 'release' too. But because we are unable to 'run away', we feel trapped and vulnerable, and the primordial part of our brain is convinced we are going to die! Now if you add to this the instinctive reaction to having suffered abuse of some form, the likelihood is that these feelings are going to be amplified and even cause flashbacks to the events where you were unable to defend yourself and get away.

Fortunately, by employing some powerful exercises to access the mistaken assumptions of not being good enough (or that it was his fault) and the consequential coping skills Jerry took on as a result of this traumatic event, he was able to change his beliefs, adopt new empowering life strategies and work through his fears. His nerves of terror turned to excitement as he confidently shared his presentation and felt even prouder when he won the contract.

Even though subconscious and unconscious beliefs are more hidden, they have more power than conscious ones. The *Titanic* was sunk not by the part of the iceberg that was visible but by the part that was invisible, hidden below the sea's surface. So, too, your hidden patterns are likely to sink your success.

Exercise: It's Never Too Late to Have a Happy Childhood

In this Root Causes exercise, we can use questions like these to root out those early misconceptions:

Find a current situation that is causing you stress, anxiety or frustration.

What is happening to cause that? What are the beliefs you are holding?

Now put your attention where you are feeling that emotion in your body.

Ask yourself:

1. 'If I were to guess what age I was when I first felt this, it was probably at the age of _____'. (Trust your first answer.)

2. 'If I were to guess who was involved and what was happening, it might have been _____'. (Trust your answers.)
3. 'If I were to guess what I probably took on as a belief, it might have been _____'.
4. The need I wasn't getting met was _____.
5. Therefore, the coping skill/vow I adopted was _____.

Now revisit that younger part of you, let him/her know that was not the truth and then change the belief. See yourself giving him/her what she needed at the time and choose to adopt a new empowering coping skill.

Forgive everything and everyone (including yourself) for the situation.

This should help to bring about a whole new layer of peace.

Perfection from Imperfection

I was working with Rose one day, planning a workshop that she was about to deliver, when she received an email from one of the participants. There was only two days to go, and Rose had already made and paid for all the extensive travel arrangements, from trains to car hire, plus hotels and refreshments for the workshop and the venue.

Rose had been meticulous in her planning, as she wanted this workshop to be perfect. She had diligently been sending informative emails to the participants and kept in touch regularly with the co-organiser.

As she read the email, I could see Rose getting more and more upset and angry. This participant was questioning the cost of the workshop and couldn't see the value so wanted to cancel not only her own place but was also going to suggest to the other participants to scrap the whole thing altogether.

Naturally, Rose's first response was to be livid. She was aghast at the audacity of this woman. 'How dare she be so disrespectful. I have sent out numerous emails, and now, two days before the event, she questions everything about the workshop'.

Rose's next reaction was to reply to this woman's email. She attempted not to sound angry in her response, to try to keep everything factual and stay firm with her boundaries that the workshop place would still have to be paid for. If the woman didn't wish to attend, she would have to find a replacement, as cancelling the whole workshop at this late stage was not an option.

Rose's 'planning to perfection' was challenged at every level and now her own self-value.

I managed to see the email before she sent it and suggested adding a paragraph of understanding where this woman might be coming from. Reluctantly, Rose tried to see it from this woman's point of view. She empathised with her about the cost, recognising that getting value for money was naturally very important to her. This was an innovative type of workshop and, on the surface, it would be difficult to understand the value without having experienced it. Rose even stated that if she was in this woman's shoes, she would probably have reacted the same way without knowing what the workshop really involved.

She then presented the rest of the facts, clearly, concisely and considerately.

She sent the email.

Whilst the extra paragraph helped the email go without anger, I could see Rose was not still completely at peace. 'I am trying not to be angry, and I am angry at not being able to be un-angry!' she burst out.

So, I took her through the above Root Causes exercise, and, from the questions, Rose remembered an incident when she was eight years old that had made her feel very hurt, invisible and disrespected.

I enquired what might she have vowed — Rose thought it was that she needed to stay invisible to be safe. But then when she was older, she vowed to get revenge by being disrespectful to the person who had originally upset her. Asking what her real need was, she answered 'To be seen and heard'.

We worked with healing the real emotions of this problem and then to complete the session, I asked where she was keeping herself invisible, not listening to herself and how she was disrespecting HERSELF.

We explored a few extra areas that sprung to mind and how this pattern had leaked out in the drama of the email. Without making herself wrong, there were several areas Rose felt she could have done differently that might have prevented receiving the email in the first place.

Once she realised that, it was 'perfect' that she received the woman's email. Rose was now able to set clearer boundaries, be aware of other people's perspectives and ensure no assumptions were made so that the next workshop would be even more successful.

Incidentally, once the woman had extra clarity, she was very willing to pay, signed up and had a great day. On greeting Rose in the morning, she was extremely apologetic and they both shared a hug — a demonstration of finding perfection in the imperfection, the right out of the wrong, respect out of the disrespect.

'Nothing happens to us that is not happening for us'.

For your free bonus content go to www.imperfectasiam.today

CHAPTER 7

Letting Go of the Reins of Control

When you are in control, you don't need to be.
Let go and trust, and you will be very happy.

—WENDYISM

Perfectionism (I'mperfectionism) is the epitome of your need for control.

The fear that you might get something wrong haunts you daily. You become addicted to feeling not good enough. Now everything in your life is about trying to be in control. As your grip tightens externally, the more out of control you feel internally. Ironically, because of your patterning and beliefs around being imperfect, perfectionism now controls you.

If you think about most types of coping strategies, for example, procrastination, addictions, perfectionism, self-harming, eating disorders, OCD, falling into debt, always being late or excessively early, hoarding, being untidy and so on — they are all about controlling outcomes that employ tactics such as disrespect, delay, distraction, doubt and denial. All the above are used to quell the anxiety of being unable to control situations and people.

That which you are trying to control is controlling you.

Everything becomes about control. When you are not in control of your life, you need certainty, predictability, little or no change. However, the very nature of these beasts will force you to have to let go sooner or later. You are being controlled by the very thing that you are trying to control. When you think you are in control of your emotions, it's the emotions controlling you. Have you noticed that when you are trying to control money, it seems the debts get higher, bills come in unexpectedly or something happens to force you to let go of it? As you desperately try to feel in control of your life, does it seem that your health, your energy and your self-esteem suffer? All of these are evidence that you are secretly out of control somewhere in your life.

Control Dramas

Previously we have explored how to create self-love. This is now going to be your real armour in overcoming the control dramas. When you don't feel good enough as you are, it is either very easy to get swayed in arguments so that you don't upset anyone or you feel you must fight to be right. You are desperate to prove your way is the right way. Remember though, anything you must prove means you don't truly believe it.

How can you know that to be true?

Because when you are authentically confident in yourself, loving who you are, you cannot be derailed by people with a different outlook. Your worth isn't determined by someone else's opinion or your fear of being disliked.

Have you ever had someone argue their viewpoint against something you posted on social media? They probably tried so hard to convince you that what you had written was wrong — and that they were right. It can be really frustrating when somebody doesn't understand your viewpoint. Essentially, do you want to be right or happy? Why waste your energy on someone who is trying to prove that $1 + 2 = 4$? You know it's only 3, so why would you give your power away?

> *For those who believe, no proof is necessary.*
> *For those who don't believe, no proof is possible.*
> —STUART CHASE

However, this doesn't mean giving in just for a quiet life. Standing up for yourself is not fighting. Fighting for your needs carries an energy of anger, demand and being off-centre. Think of the martial arts. The skill is always to stay centred, especially when the other person is attacking. If you are both attacking, then you will both end up losing in some way. Keep your calm and continue to state your needs with kindness.

Power Struggles

'But if I am calm, I feel my partner has power over me because I can't shout at him', one of my clients exclaimed.

Jane was with a partner who tried her patience no end with his untidiness. She could not get him to do what she wanted. No matter how much she bribed, cajoled and threatened, she could not get her needs met, even though she asked him and pleaded with him again and again! To say she was frustrated was an understatement.

If you are confronted with unwillingness from the other person, this can often be the result of a hidden power struggle going on between you. Nobody likes to feel their power is being taken from them, which is why, when you demand that your needs be met, you will be confronted with huge resistance. An interesting observation is that often the very thing you are demanding the other person give to you is what you are not giving to yourself.

In a healthy relationship, asking for your needs to be met should be received with willingness. If it's not, again in a healthy relationship, there is permission to say no. So, if they are resisting you, maybe your lesson is to learn how to be willing to hear 'no'. If they are frequently saying 'no', can you discover what is preventing them from saying 'yes'?

As mentioned in earlier chapters, when you are meeting your own needs, in essence, you won't keep demanding others give you what you are not giving yourself.

Back to Jane. There are several real reasons why Jane was so upset. Exploring these through the lens of the journey you have been on with this book will provide you with a way to logically process a similar situation that may arise for you. Think of someone you might be experiencing something similar with and play along using the same questions.

1. What is the belief you are holding about the person or event?

In Jane's case, she strongly held the belief that her partner did not and would not meet her needs. As you learned previously, this becomes a script for the other person; they are assigned the role that they will not meet your needs in your movie of life. So naturally, they don't! Because of this, Jane could only ever see her partner NOT meeting her needs; even if he DID want to, he couldn't (unless he had the higher-consciousness awareness that he was caught up in her script — most of us don't know we are). Such is the power of scripts and beliefs. First, Jane needs to change her perception of her partner, change her belief about him and mentally visualise him meeting her needs and then believe he will be willing to do this.

Q. Who do you need to change your perception or belief about?

2. What is the reflection?

Jane's partner MUST be mirroring something back to her (and vice versa). If Jane is seeing him not meeting her needs, the question she would have to ask herself is, 'Where am I not meeting my own needs?'

Q. What could your challenging person be reflecting to you about you?

3. What is the emotion?

When someone does or does not do something you want, in the way that you want, it will create an emotional response in you — usually anger — because you can't control them. This means either you already have that emotion within you that needs healing or, quite often, because you are an easy target, that person can use you to siphon off their own anger. In other words, they seem to stay calm and you behave like a raging madman! This is how you are being controlled by them. Jane's partner knew consciously (or unconsciously) how to push her buttons and so he didn't have to feel the anger that Jane readily and consistently reacted with.

Q. Which emotional button is someone pushing and controlling in you?

4. What is the fear?

Jane knew in her heart of hearts that her partner wasn't going to change, and so she had to face her fear that if, despite requesting her needs to be met (in calm ways, with clear boundaries) where she needed support and help, her partner still had absolutely no desire to support her, then in order to keep her self-respect and self-esteem intact, she would need to consider leaving him. In a healthy loving relationship, there is a natural willingness to want to support one another, meet one another's needs and do what you can to help that partner feel loved and happy. No one is trying to control anyone.

Q. What/who do you fear losing control of?

5. How are you asking and communicating?

Without realising it, when you are a perfectionist you are always demanding your needs are met — your way. This will cause a natural resistance because nobody likes being told what to do or have demands made of them.

Instead of demanding her partner meet her needs, Jane needed to find a way to empathise with his needs first, one of which was to relax after a hard day, but also ask if he would be willing to help her do x y z. Most times when communication comes as a request, *balanced* people are willing to help. If they say 'no', you need to respect that they do have that right. Decide what is important to you. Is there a different way this need could be met? If they repeatedly say 'no', then you may have to take an honest look at the relationship.

Q. Are you requesting or demanding?

6. Where have you first felt this or experienced something like this?

Earlier we explored how events in our childhood create beliefs and scripts that follow us through life. When I worked with Jane, we discovered that when she was six, she needed help with something from her father, but he totally dismissed her. Unconsciously she took on the belief that she wasn't worth having her needs met and, even more so, that men didn't meet her needs.

Being unaware of this old patterning, Jane often attracted people, including partners, who seemed to have no option but to act out this self-fulfilling prophecy.

With Jane, we worked at discovering what her original need was, which incidentally was love and affection, and how she could give that love and affection to herself now. Next, she had to visualise going back in time and meeting that need for the younger part of her — and changing those outdated beliefs!

Q. What was the significant event in your life that shaped your beliefs and created a need for control?

7. What are you controlling that needs releasing?

As discussed earlier, when you are seeking perfection, the belief that you do not feel good enough is so strong that you need to control everything and everyone in some way. Unfortunately, this can often make other people feel not good enough in your company, so they will seek to keep some control around you.

In Jane's case, her need for everything to be perfect around her was driving her partner away as he felt he couldn't relax in his own home. This had the adverse effect of making him even untidier, as this was his way of keeping some form of control in his own already stressed-out life.

Eventually, after coaching Jane through these steps, she realised how much resistance was coming from her partner because of her obsessiveness and OCD-ness, which led her to attempt to control everything and everyone. Once she was able to let go of some of her unrealistic expectations, she began to find a way to communicate what she really wanted to her partner. He became more willing to support her because she stopped demanding he meet her needs, and consequently they found a way to start sorting the situation out.

Once Jane realised that her need to control her partner was a symptom of her being out of control in her own life (which also contributed to an eating disorder), she stopped trying to control him, resulting in healthier conversations between them.

Q. Who do you need to stop trying to control or stop allowing to control you?

From Relationship Breakdowns to Relationship Breakthroughs

When you can quit the power struggles and control dramas, even if there has been a relationship breakdown, this can be a fantastic opportunity to have a breakthrough. The key here is to look at what part you have played in the breakdown.

Most breakdowns are due to unrealistic expectations of perfection from a partner. Too often, when you are not feeling good enough inside, you will unconsciously project that onto other people. They now become the ones not good enough. Remember, 'If you spot it, you got it'.

What you are condemning them for is what you are condemning yourself for. When you are willing to find the real need under the demand, then you can learn to request your need in a more kind, loving and respectful way. In my experience, most people want to love, support or help; however, they don't like being put upon, taken for granted or feeling they have no choice. When you can be very clear in your communication, and combine this with your new level of self-love, you will find a whole new level of cooperation.

If, after all that grounding, self-awareness and self-love you don't get your need met, then either it was meant to come from someone else, yourself, or maybe it is time to look at the true integrity of the relationship.

This was Jane's final step.

How to Let Go of Control but Feel in Charge

This principle leads you to feeling more in control of yourself, which in turn gives you the courage to let go of power struggles and take back your power. This will give you a feeling of being perfectly in charge without necessarily needing to control everything and everyone. To do this, you have to be prepared for your idea of perfection to not necessarily be the right thing for you or anyone. The bigger the need for perfection and control, the more your lesson is to 'Relax and Let Go'. If you find this difficult, then revisit the 'So what then?' exercise in Chapter 4.

> *Perfect right action is always taking place.*
> *So, it's time to let go of control and embrace.*
> —WENDYISM

For your free bonus content go to www.imperfectasiam.today

CHAPTER 8

The Silent Saboteur of Success

When you have lost hope, it can be difficult to cope;
Rest assured that whatever you are going through,
Source is right there with you!

—WENDYISM

The Stress of Success

She had just celebrated her best-ever summer. Bookings were up, bills were paid and, for the first time in ages, financially she was ahead. She even had a great team that were working effectively and harmoniously together — for a change!

Everything was finally on track when, one day, one of her customers told her that they wanted to buy their daughter a pony, but they only wanted to keep it on DIY grass livery ('Do It Yourself' is the cheapest way to keep a pony). For her business, this is the least profitable income stream there is. Going completely against her intuition and gut feeling, and because she could not bear to say no to people, she agreed.

Unknown to everyone, this pony had strangles (a highly contagious disease that affects horses in a bad way). Unfortunately, the pony was what is called a silent carrier (in other words, showing no symptoms initially). It wasn't long before several other horses were infected and, because of the seriousness of the disease, the yard had to go into lockdown, resulting in a serious loss of business. A partial blessing was that she was insured, but because one of the ponies was seriously ill and therefore required ongoing expensive veterinary treatment, it wasn't long before the amount provided by the insurers was used up.

The good news is that the pony recovered, the business reopened and she started making headway again. But then BOOM, it happened again! Her yard got hit by a second bout of strangles. Once again, a friend of hers had been desperate to find a place for her own pony, and yet again — going against her intuitive feeling and gut sense not to — the pretty little pony arrived at her yard. This time precautions had been put in place, and the pony subsequently spent a month in quarantine. But, again, unbeknown to her, he too was another silent carrier. It was only when the pony started to get really stressed that the strangles virus leaked out. More ponies were infected, and the business had to close AGAIN. More losses.

Then the big one hit.

Fast-forward a year. The horses had recovered, business was improving and life seemed to be getting back on an even keel.

However, at 5 a.m. on July 12, 2017, the phone rang.

'Quick, you need to get here; your barn is on fire!' shouted her neighbour. Without time to dress properly, she slung a jumper over her jimjams, grabbed her coat and boots, and drove like a maniac to her stables, only to see most of the buildings engulfed in flames. Fire engines had started to arrive, but her only thought was for the horses. Fortunately, her neighbour had released the horses that were stabled, but there were still some in the top paddocks and these were being affected by the smoke. Frantically she and her neighbour managed to grab hold of these horses and lead them to a field further away. All the horses were safe, Thank God — literally.

Upon returning to the stables, she discovered that there were now fifteen fire engines fighting the fire — all of these were necessary due to there not being enough water supply in the rural area where she lived.

She watched helplessly as everything she owned for the horses and stables went up in flames. The hay, the feed, the rugs, the tractor, the quad bike, her husband's fifty-year-old collection of maintenance tools. The only saving grace was that the actual physical stables were saved, and the tack room, thankfully, located in a separate part of the yard, was undamaged. She stared in utter despair and disbelief as the flames licked higher and higher into the night sky ...

Although you may have changed your limiting beliefs and healed some emotions, you might well find there still seems something that is sabotaging you and won't quite let you get to the next level.

What is blocking you from manifesting what you really want?

Why does it appear that progress is slowing down, or mistakes seem to keep happening and you feel you are back to square one, even though you have put so much effort into changing your life?

This is the 'temptation period'. To go back to feeling imperfect, not good enough, and start blaming yourself for why things go wrong. Lo and behold, the I'mperfectionism syndrome kicks in again alongside all those patterns you thought you had healed!

It is now time to explore where there may still be some unconscious vows, mixed messages or crossed wires disrupting your efforts. Not understanding why you have these hidden blocks can cause the patterns of procrastination, perfectionism and other limiting behaviours to reignite. The effect on your life is like going to a well with a colander. The energy leaks need plugging.

Moreover, refusing to deal with emotional energy leaks (from unhealed traumas or buried feelings) can result in firing up your internal saboteur to cause complete havoc with your life.

If your money story seems to have taken a dive, you need to look at your financial and success thermostats. There is probably a 'setpoint' that won't allow you to keep the new level of wealth, health and happiness you have worked so hard to achieve.

Sealing Energy Leaks

For every unfinished project, unread book, incomplete course, unhealed trauma, unforgiven person or unfelt feeling, even unread email, there is a cord of energy that attaches you to it or them. This is exactly like having multiple tabs and apps open on your 'neck-top computer'. Just as this would severely slow your computer down, so too will your success slacken off, or your own energy will be completely depleted. Because you have not brought completion or closure to these situations, your mind has logged these on its 'still-to-do' list. Just because you have forgotten all about it doesn't mean your immaculate memory has.

Why Does This Matter?

When you have unfinished business, your mind keeps a tally and uses the SAME energy as if you were still doing it AND uses a lot of energy to RESIST doing it, which is why, when you are a procrastinator, you always feel so tired — even though you are NOT doing what you think will exhaust you TO do! Your energy bucket turns into a colander, and all your precious energy leaks out. The ways these energy leaks could show up in your life would be in the form of lost opportunities, success coming very slowly, overwhelm, overweight (your body is trying to fill the holes and this is probably why you feel empty all the time), underweight (you have not replaced the energy that is leaking out), depression, illnesses, disease, pain, procrastination, perfectionism, loss of confidence, loss of joy, loss of purpose, loss of creativity, debts, bankruptcy, divorce and so on.

Hence the expression 'It takes more energy to NOT do something'.

When we have unhealed traumas, hurts, angers, sadnesses and other buried feelings (in addition to the *practical* things we have unfinished business with), this exhausts us further because of the enormous levels of energy needed to keep those emotions in check.

Ironically, one of the other ways we try to avoid these feelings or traumas is by becoming a perfectionist. The fear of tapping into an old feeling or traumatic event again that led us to feeling not good enough is so huge that we avoid doing it by busying ourselves and demanding perfection — from ourselves and others. This attempt at avoidance of getting something wrong, making a mistake or getting someone's disapproval becomes an obsession and, unchecked, can lead to OCD, addictions or other obsessive behaviours, in order to quell the anxiety and fear.

The more you avoid healing traumatic events and past upsets, the more likely you will attract vicious self-sabotage. If you have been so enraged but have not had a safe space to be heard or healed, that hurt part of you will pop up into your life when you least expect it and cause havoc.

Take a moment and start making a list using several sheets of paper.

Here are some examples:

Sheet 1   All the projects you have going on now.
Sheet 2   All the courses you have bought but not completed.
Sheet 3   All the books you have bought but not read. (If you are anything like me, you may need several sheets for this one!)
Sheet 4   Everyone who is still upsetting you, you are angry with or don't have closure with, or the emotions you don't want to feel or are trying to bury.
Sheet 5   All the traumas you have been through.
Sheet 6   Make a note of the number of unread emails.
Sheet 7   All the rooms in your home that need decluttering.

You will need quite a bit of time to do this, so plan when you can be undisturbed. You may have to allocate a certain time each day to go through the lists.

Sheet 1. To Do or Not to Do!

Start with the sheet that feels most manageable. Maybe the projects you have going on right now.

When I had over twenty-six projects, my coach got me to assign them to one of four boxes:

- Urgent courses to complete
- Important accreditations
- Not-urgent books to read
- Not-important

By putting it in chart form, you can see what is urgent and important and what is not urgent or important.

Here are some ideas with things that you might need sorting:

TO DO OR NOT TO DO	Important	Not Important
Urgent	Send important documents off. Make phone calls for the business. Complete new website. Any projects that would help your business!	Finish decorating the kitchen. Complete course taken. Update LinkedIn profile/CV.
Not Urgent	Declutter the garage. Speak to the person who upset you. Heal the past. Sort bills.	Sort email list. Finish/start books that need reading. Clean the car.

Assign each to a box, depending on its importance or urgency. This restored an enormous amount of energy and enthusiasm for me. Instead of sitting in the overwhelm, anxiety and procrastination, I was able to create a sense of order and clarity regarding what was important or urgent to me. I had to decide to do it, delegate it or drop it.

Sheet 2. Incomplete Courses

Look at your list of incomplete courses. Which ones do you absolutely know you are not going to finish, that you have no interest in or aren't really that important to you anymore?

With each of these courses, you can either gift it to someone who will finish it (if you have the copyright permission) or delete it with the conscious statement 'I choose not to complete this course and am choosing to release this completely'. This is an important declaration to make your mind cease spending all the energy required to remember the course needs completing.

Place any remaining courses in order of importance, commit to start doing something with each of them or choose one course and put all your energy into completing it. Perhaps allocate a certain day or time that you absolutely keep sacred.

If so, use one of the following statements: 'I am choosing to complete this course on _____'. Or 'I am completing this course on _____'. Follow through with your commitment.

The great thing is that it's not about the amount of time you allocate to doing the course but the fact you are doing something that tells your subconscious you ARE doing the course. This allows your energy to start flowing but not leak. You will start to feel energised rather than energy drained.

Sheet 3. Books

Plugging this leak can be overwhelming if you are a bookaholic like me and, again, it may need to be done in stages. However, it's important to remember that everything you own carries a cord of energy to it. Everything unfinished or unread leaks energy. That energy is always trying to be replaced. If you have only a few books, this will be relatively easy, but if you have an enormous collection, then break this exercise up into bite-size pieces timewise, so that you do not become overwhelmed.

To begin with, go through your books and decide which ones you absolutely cannot throw away, that are sacred to you. I must confess some of my early books are like old friends — they helped me get through a very difficult period of my life. Maybe allocate a special bookcase for them. Thank the author and the words and be clear to mind: 'I have read these books, and I choose to keep them'.

Next, decide on the books you could give away. Is there someone you know who could really benefit from any of them? Which ones can you donate to charity? Or you can even make some money and sell them to secondhand book organisations like Ziffit or World of Books (they take CDs and PlayStations too).

Finally, which ones do you really want to keep and read? Make a date with yourself and commit to a reading time, ideally daily. Almost every successful person you meet will tell you that one of the secrets to their success is 'daily learning'. Start implementing a 'power hour' that consists of twenty minutes each of meditation, exercise and reading. 'When you learn you earn'. Or, instead of watching TV in the evening, spend some time reading.

So, read, get rid of or repurpose.

Sheet 4. People Still Upsetting Me

Essentially you are looking at what in the other person's behaviour upsets you.

Create two columns:

Column 1: What is it about their behaviour that upsets me?
Column 2: Where do I do that — either to myself or others?

If you have difficulty with this, reread Chapter 2 to help you remember the Law of Reflection.

Now forgive them and yourself (see Chapter 9 for more understanding of forgiveness).

Sheet 5. Traumatic Events

Go through this list and, as you look back, notice which events still trigger you with upset feelings. These are the feelings to heal.

- Find the belief behind them.
- What was the coping skill you adopted?
- Is that still serving you? If not, change it.
- What was the real need that wasn't met?
- In what way can you give that need to yourself now? Unmet needs of the past always show up as a need you are not giving yourself in the present.
- Finally, what have been the positives of this experience? How has it helped your life? If you are still in the pain of the event, this could be the way out. Remember, nothing happens *to* you that is not happening *for* you.

You either use the past to be a stumbling block with pain or use it as a springboard for joy and gifts to gain.
—WENDYISM

When you can reach the feeling of gratitude for the experience, you have reached complete healing and understanding of its purpose.

Sheet 6. Unread Emails

Okay, hands up. I haven't completely mastered this one yet personally, and I am sure there are some better ways to handle them. This is a non-techy Wendy way. What I have been doing is using 'TV time' to delete unwanted emails. I bring up all the emails from a specific person and then quickly scan to see if there is anything important. I then unsubscribe if they are not essential to my business, then delete all emails from that person. Finally, I create a folder for anything important.

As I've said, there are probably better ways to manage this, but the key is doing SOMETHING about them, rather than your mind (and body) having to use precious energy remembering there are 26,000 'unread' emails in your inbox to read! (And that was just *one* of my email addresses!)

Sheet 7. Clutter (the Opposite Side to Home Perfectionism)

Confession time. I am still very much a work in progress with this one, so I don't feel I have the right to offer much advice yet. There are so many brilliant books, YouTube videos, courses and Facebook groups that can help you much better than I can. What I *can* help you with is the understanding of the relevance of clutter, chaos and carnage.

They are all symptoms of stress, unhealed traumas, buried emotions and the need to be *in* control of what is feeling *out* of control in your life, either now or when you have had a serious loss of control in the past.

If you are a serious clutteraholic, you need to work on releasing the traumas of your past, first, or even in tandem, as you clear. Once you can release the emotions associated with the trauma, it will be easier to release the clutter and you will start feeling lighter and gain more clarity in your life.

Chaos can also represent not being clear regarding what you really want for your life. Chapter 10 has some great exercises to assist with this.

With all of these exercises, the key is to seal the energy leaks which are probably sabotaging your life and your success.

The Sabotage Setpoint

Have you ever noticed when you have a pay raise your bills seem to increase, or if you get a bonus or windfall, almost immediately an unexpected expense appears? Maybe you have just cleared your credit cards and suddenly a major repair is necessary for your home or car!

Multiple studies show that 70 percent of lottery winners go broke within the first five years. Seventy percent! Why is that? I believe you can't get past your financial setpoint without conscious support.

What is a financial setpoint? You know how the heating thermostat in your home works. You set the room temperature to, say, 20°C. The boiler in the background gets to work to ensure the room reaches 20°C, and any time it starts dropping below, it kicks in to maintain the 20°C. However, if the room starts getting too warm, the boiler stops producing heat and will not come on until the temperature has fallen below 20°C.

This is sort of how your financial setpoint works. You have 'set' your monthly income to, say, £2K and there are a few small ups and downs, ebbs and flows, but as soon as your income jumps much higher than that, your thermostat kicks in to bring that net income back down through bills, disasters, repairs, etc.

What influences your financial setpoint? Your self-worth, your family paradigm (family beliefs about money you inherited), sacred vows or contracts made as a child ('I won't be more successful than my parents' is an example), embarrassment, feeling unsafe with money, beliefs about rich people. One of the biggest reasons your saboteur kicks in is because of unhealed trauma, along with your buried emotions.

To go beyond the financial setpoint takes a lot of conscious healing work, establishing new beliefs, releasing old emotions and creating new behaviours and coping skills. This is better done with a coach who understands financial setpoints (press link www.theheartcentreuk.com for my online course on how to raise your financial setpoint).

… The cost of the fire damage was over £100K, and although some of it was covered by insurance, she came to recognise this was the ultimate act of self-sabotage of years of hard work and success. As she watched the raging flames, she knew something had to change about the secret rage she had been carrying from her childhood. She had to seek help to heal. She could no longer do this on her own.

So, I did seek proper help and healing, and things did change!

Non-action creates procrastination,
procrastination creates stagnation,
stagnation creates exhaustion.

Action creates traction,
traction creates energy,
energy creates flow,
flow creates dough!
—WENDYISM

For your free bonus content go to www.imperfectasiam.today

CHAPTER 9

Let Go of the Past to Free Yourself for the Future

You can't go forwards if you are looking backwards.
—WENDYISM

One of my clients, Jennifer, was an amazing intellect. Her list of accreditations, degrees, and so on was so long they could have gone on a toilet roll. The brainiest person I had ever known, yet she could not get over the fact she had failed at her marriage, which left her feeling unsuccessful and 'not good enough'! No matter what she did or didn't do for her husband, she couldn't make him happy.

Using the feeling of failure, we delved a bit deeper using the Root Cause exercise (see Chapter 6) and discovered that at the age of seven, Jennifer had come second in class and, although she was pleased, when she went home, her dad was disappointed that she hadn't come first. This led her to believe that, unless she got everything 'perfect', she would not receive love and would be a disappointment. This led to a lifetime of trying to prove she wasn't a failure. But because her attention was always about trying to prove she wasn't, the feeling intensified, and no matter how many external validations she received, she could never stop feeling a failure. This belief, being so strong, drew events to her like her marriage failing and her business and financial life never being the true success they should have been, considering the number of distinguished qualifications she had.

By finally freeing herself from the past with forgiveness, particularly around her dad, and forgiving herself for never believing she was good enough, she found the masses of gifts she gained from this past scenario. She then started focusing on just how much of a success she was and has been. Her career turned a corner, she released herself from the belief she had failed at her marriage and finally financial flow started coming in, reflecting her expertise. Jennifer was finally freed from her prison of perfectionism.

Where might you still be holding on to the past in the way of incomplete projects, being a busyaholic, procrastinating? Maybe there are people in your past you are struggling to forgive. Whatever is coming up as adverse experiences — the troublesome person you are dealing with, success still eluding you — gives you clues that there is still a past trauma, belief or behaviour that needs releasing. Let us explore some practical ways to truly let go of the past so that you can fully feel free for the future.

Why Part of You Won't Let Go or Change

'Well, if I knew that, I would have let go by now', I am guessing you are probably saying. Even after over thirty years of studying the human psyche, I still find it fascinating that letting go of past painful situations is quite a challenge for most people (I include myself too). Logically, our adult brain can process that the past is over, the threat is over or that the people and situation involved were all going through stuff too.

However, we are very seldom operating from our adult self. Most times it's one of our younger selves that hasn't really grown up. When you have a traumatic experience, the emotion of that event often gets stuck in your body, especially shock.

Nearly all the I'mperfectionists I have personally worked with have been through some sort of trauma in their past. No matter how much healing, letting go and moving on with your life you may have done, if you are not getting the success you deserve in your life, there's still some further releasing, healing or understanding needed. This is likely to be something or someone that needs forgiveness in some way.

Let's do some digging …

Exercise: Freedom Day

Step 1. Who, What, Why?

List the key people who have made you angry, hurt, upset or who have betrayed or rejected you, and then write down everyone and everything that annoys you about people not getting things right, making mistakes and not doing their job properly, and why this annoys you.

Now list all the projects/courses you haven't completed or opportunities you didn't take, and why.

Step 2. If You Were to Know _____

What was it about what they did that upset/hurt you? Pick out keywords and jot them down.

Why does it annoy you when others get it wrong?

Why did you not complete those projects or take those opportunities? What was the fear?

Step 3. Where in You Am I?

Look back over your list and ask yourself, 'Where have I done something similar to others or, more likely, to myself?' (You may have not exactly done it in the same way or form but in essence.)

Step 4. Mirror, Mirror

Find a mirror and, starting with the top of your list, look in the mirror and say, 'The person I most need to forgive is _____ (name) for _____.'

Keep doing this until everyone on your list has been forgiven.

Then work on the part of your list that is about you, and forgive yourself for everything and everywhere you have done something similar to others or yourself.

'I forgive myself for _____.'

Step 5. Find the Need, Heal the Deed!

Look back over your lists and find what was the real need that others didn't give you and what was the real need you were trying to get met by being perfect or procrastinating. (For example, by trying to be perfect, did you want someone's acceptance? By procrastinating, did you want reassurance that it was okay to not get it right?)

Step 6. Give to Yourself

Now explore how you can meet that need in yourself. In what way could you give yourself reassurance, acceptance and love? (Or whatever your real need was.)

States and Stages of Understanding Forgiveness

There are a lot of layers to forgiveness, and the above process is just one of those stages. The key point for this chapter is to understand the benefit of releasing the past or even present frustrations, hurts and anger in the form of forgiveness.

The first thing to recognise is that forgiveness is not about condoning people's actions or inactions. In the physical world, you will still have to maintain boundaries and take necessary steps and actions to prevent the behaviour. However, the key point is that forgiveness is about letting go of the feeling.

All the while you are hanging on to the past through continuing to feel hurt, angry or rejected, and so on, your power for the present moment gets taken away. Your energy is leaking like a sieve. This is one of the key reasons success could be eluding you.

As said earlier, emotions and feelings are just energy in motion. But every bit of lack of forgiveness is like you having a cord of energy linking to the other person and all your power is being siphoned off.

Non-forgiveness of others doesn't affect them, but it does affect you. That cord is not plugged, so there is still energy leaking out of you.

The Innocent Pays for the Guilty

Another important fact is to recognise that when you are holding on to your resentments, guilts and frustrations towards others, that emotional energy emanating from you *must* go through the innocent people in your life — your children, your pets, your partner, your work colleagues, your family, your friends and, in business, even your clients.

Even your own body can be innocently affected by all your toxic emotions. Holding on to emotions can create illnesses and diseases as well as financial problems. It can also sabotage success and cause relationship issues.

Forgiveness Restarts Your Life

One of the best advantages of forgiveness is that it restarts your life. One of the most common effects is that you feel lighter, freer and happier. Your creativity and inspiration are unleashed, your finances flow, your opportunities increase, your health improves, relationships become more rewarding and the people in your life respond differently towards you — in a good way.

Self-Forgiveness Is the Ultimate Gift

The act of being willing to completely release the past and forgive yourself for any perceived mistakes, guilts or failures is the single most important gift of self-love and self-care you can give to yourself. When you feel so much better about yourself, your life can really take off. So, is there anything else stopping you?

Your Past Invades the Now

Louisa was just one of these people. She had been working with me for a while, overcoming her OCD-ness, and had the realisation that this had kicked in after she had been raped. We had really shifted a lot of 'stuff' over the course of our sessions together and had even done loads of forgiveness work. But it seemed there was still something we could never quite get to the bottom of. Unfortunately, it was affecting her ability to feel safe with any new partners.

One of the ways I work is by combining my HEART Therapeutic Coaching with the assistance of horses to elicit even deeper issues and insights. We were working outside, and Caesar, the horse Louisa was working with, got startled and wanted to run away. As we were in a safe paddock, Louisa let the horse loose and allowed him to run around. As we were watching him, the subject came up about how horses naturally *still* want to run *after* something has frightened them. What that does is to physically help release the emotional trauma and fear from their bodies. We then realised that, in Louisa's past traumatic situation, she had never been able to get away from her perpetrator. Watching Caesar gave us an idea: Louisa would lie down on the ground and simulate her past traumatic situation, but this time she would change the ending. I placed an improvised heavyish object on top of her. Louisa closed her eyes and took herself back to the moment just before she was raped. This time she was able to say 'No!' by screaming at the perpetrator to stop and then pushed 'him' off and got up and ran and ran and ran around the paddock we were in. Naturally, there were a lot of tears, but the relief she felt in her body was utterly amazing.

Meanwhile, Caesar, who was still loose, had been watching Louisa run around. Once she had stopped, completely of his own volition, he came over to her and nuzzled into her. It was as though a mutual recognition of past trauma had occurred. There were even more tears from both of us at this poignant moment.

If you are still not sure if you have baggage from the past affecting you, take a moment to review what is going on in your life. Are there situations still causing you anxiety? Do you suddenly get triggers that set off an addiction? Maybe you just can't seem to shake that depression. Often your body and subconscious mind could still be stuck in the past. Perhaps you have had something traumatic happen but, despite doing all the usual beneficial exercises, something continues to hold you back.

One of the reasons this was such a powerful exercise for Louisa is that she had symbolically been able to 'change the ending' of her story. Now of course, she will never be able to physically change what happened, but because the unconscious mind works in pictures and metaphors, and the body holds cellular memory and emotions, this empowering enactment of emotional release sent the message to the unconscious mind that Louisa was able to stop the rape and get away. The unconscious mind does not really know fact from fiction. The most important part of this exercise was the sense of relief Louisa felt as she ran, releasing years of emotional and traumatic memories from the cells of her body.

From Victim to Victor

To complete the session and really move on from the past, we sat down and looked at all the ways this event shaped Louisa as a person and got her to where she is today. We found loads of positives and 'If it wasn't for …' moments and, although she would not want that event ever to be repeated, the biggest gift Louisa received, together with the insight she gained, allowed her to take this life experience and heal others who have been or are going through something similar. She could now be a victor, not a victim.

We took the forgiveness up a final notch, which was to recognise that, from a higher level of consciousness, there was nothing to forgive. The biggest bonus she gained was being able to relax about everything having to be perfect and in her control (which, ironically, made her feel out of control), and this in turn allowed Louisa to truly feel in charge of her life. A little footnote to add is that not long after this magical session, Louisa started to go out with a lovely man who, interestingly, had been 'in the wings' in her life for quite a while beforehand, but she had never been able to feel safe enough to engage with him.

In what way could you change the ending of your story? How could you take yourself from victim to victor? You have that power.

The Titanic Sank — Get Over It!

No matter how tragic an event has been, at some point you have to move on if you want your life to flourish. You can hang on to the illusion of control by 'trying' to be perfect and 'trying' to perfectly control every outcome and 'trying' to manipulate everything and everyone around you and 'trying' to avoid failure, rejection and disapproval, *but* at some point, you need to let the past go if you want your life to truly succeed.

Another reason it is vital to release the past — any unresolved issues, unforgiveness or refusal to see the gift from the situation — is that life has a way of recreating it to help you change the ending, rechoose and move on.

The best way I can illustrate this is from my own experience.

For years and years and even more years, I could not and would not let go of the hurt of being rejected by my dad when he went off to live with another family. To add insult to my internal injury, when I went to him for help and asked for £45 to buy a ton of hay to feed my pony—which he did give me—he made me pay him back.

What this led to was nearly fifty years of resentment towards my father and his family and, although I spent hours doing forgiveness work on him, there was just this piece I could not get past.

The belief I took on was 'I can never keep what I ask for financially, because I always have to pay it back'. And so, no matter how much I did or didn't earn, I was always in debt. Even though my mum would frequently, lovingly bail me out, it was as though that money just vanished into a big hole. It was never long before I was back in the same debt. And even though Mum never made me pay her back, my belief that 'I can't have or keep what I ask for' was stronger than the fact that I didn't have to repay her. Let me repeat that: Notice that even though there have probably been thousands of times when I asked for something and received it and did not have to pay it back (and was able to keep it), I was still not able to 'see' this evidence because of my insistence that my early belief system was right.

To illustrate this, look around your room and notice everything that is a particular colour, say, cream. Now close your eyes and, keeping them closed, remember where all the pink and green things were. More difficult, yes? Because your focus is on one thing, you can't 'see' what else is there.

How many times during the day are you always getting things right and even perfect for that moment, and yet you make ONE mistake and start beating yourself up and telling yourself you are a failure?

Holding on to this resentment for so long had other dire consequences for me. My unforgiveness towards Dad didn't affect him as much as it did my finances. Because that wounded child within me believed he owed me, all it did was create a sieve to hold my financial flow and create a lifetime of struggle and debt. Not only could I never ask for help when I really needed it (for fear of humiliation, embarrassment and shame if they said no) but also the toxicity of the anger, hurt and resentment packed tightly in my body created a huge weight problem and a hidden depression.

When I was finally able to forgive and see the real gift of what having to pay Dad back helped me with through my life, I was able to finally free myself of this inner torture and ultimately a form of self-harm in continuing to be hurt.

Although I set myself up for a lifetime of struggle and became a child-preneur at the age of twelve, finding innovative ways to keep my pony, that determination created resilience and tenacity all through my life. It's now time to allow myself to receive the real rewards, revenue and recognition for all the hard work I have put in throughout life.

When you are willing to find the gifts behind the pain, you will come to realise the highest forgiveness principle — there is nothing and no one to forgive. Everything and everyone were acting in Divine Right Order, and so your past was perfect.

When you truly let go of the past,
your life will move forward very fast!
—WENDYISM

For your free bonus content go to www.imperfectasiam.today

CHAPTER 10

The Gift of the Present

All that you seek outside of you, you will never find,
in phone checking, Facebook or other addiction kind.
Instead, take time to go within,
to find yourself and the Infinite Divine.

—WENDYISM

Having received the tools for healing the past and letting go of your sabotaging stories, you are now in a position to really raise your vibration. By discovering the power of feeling connected, giving yourself time and focusing on what is truly important for your day, you are now able to make conscious choices and deliberate decisions that create the life of your dreams.

As you unite with your version of Source, Universe, God, Buddha, and the like, so you connect to flow and exciting synchronicities; 'A peace that surpasses all understanding' fills you and your life.

You have uprooted your beliefs, you have understood your reflections, you have healed your emotions, stepped through your fears, conquered your lack of confidence, learned how to change your story, discovered the Truth, sealed your energy leaks and let go of the past.

You have set yourself free from your prison cell of perfectionism. You are now standing on the outside of the gates of your penitentiary. Now what?

Now it is time to truly focus on the NOW.

What do you want?

What would you truly love for your life? Decisions, decisions, decisions …

This is the time to decide what you would love from your life. Not because you are trying to prove you ARE good enough, or that everything HAS to be perfect in case someone can find cause to reject you, or even that you are TRYING to feel worthy and deserving. But just Because. Because you are already worthy, you are already perfect as you are, and you are already deserving of every good thing in your life.

How do you discover what it is you really desire? Well, the trick is to take away any limitations of time, money, geography, talent or other people's reactions, and the like.

Exercise: The Unlimited You

In this next exercise, you yourself are unlimited and you have unlimited resources. So go grab a pen and paper, and take a moment to daydream. Once you have read the steps, you might find it even more powerful to do the exercise with your eyes closed.

- Step 1. First, imagine roots coming from your feet and going deep into the ground. Find a solid rock to let those roots anchor around.
- Step 2. Allow all your worries, tension and stress to drain out through your feet.
- Step 3. Imagine a beautiful white, golden light pouring in above you and let it 'wash' through your body, releasing any remaining worry, stress or tension. Starting from the crown of your head, through your head, neck, shoulders, arms, hands, chest, lungs,

stomach, hips, buttocks, thighs, knees, calves, ankles and toes. Finally, release it out through the roots in your feet.

- Step 4. Imagine now being able to draw renewed Life Force energy up through those roots in the same way a tree does.
- Step 5. Fast-forward yourself to sometime in the future where you have created your perfect life.
    - What are you seeing?
    - Where are you living?
    - What type of home do you have?
    - What are you doing?
    - Who is with you?
    - How does it feel to finally be financially free?
    - Really get into this 'mini-movie' and absorb the feelings of joy, freedom, love, peace, harmony and gratitude into every cell of your body.
    - Come out of the movie and jot down everything you can see, hear, feel, etc.
    - Close your eyes and feel yourself back there.
    - Now, go ask your future self:
        - 'How did I get here?'
        - 'What advice can you give me?'

Trust your answers, even if they don't make sense yet.

How did it feel to have the life you really want? Before we go into creating it, we need to just check to see if there are any remaining beliefs limiting you. What are you saying to yourself?

- 'I could never achieve that'.
- 'It's too big'.

- 'I don't deserve anything so fanciful'.

Or

- 'Wow, it's wonderful!'
- 'How do I get there?'
- 'This is what I deserve'.

If you have any little dregs of belittling beliefs, then nip back to Chapter 1 and go through the Changing Your Beliefs exercise.

You have two options now. You can either wait until you achieve that dream to feel happy, fulfilled, at peace, and so on (which I hasten to add will be a very long journey and wait because the outside of you cannot fill the inside of you), or you can fast-track by borrowing the feelings of what your new life will feel like and bring those into your present situation, i.e., 'Act as if' or 'Fake it until you make it'. Start taking action — even in small steps — towards your new life.

What is the Difference Between Being a Perfectionist and Creating a Perfect Life?

What we discovered throughout the book is that by being a perfectionist (imperfectionist), you are unlikely to be fully enjoying your life. By trying to be perfect everywhere in your life, you are probably not getting any satisfaction from anything. The emotions you are likely to be experiencing are frustration, fear or feeling a failure.

Creating your perfect life is the result of approaching it from the opposite direction. Getting into the emotions of peace, gratitude, joy and acceptance FIRST, no matter what your current situation is, transforms your life completely.

Here are some ideas on how you can start or end your day or go through the day. The more you can raise your vibration and let go of your old patterns of perfectionism, the quicker you can create your perfect life.

Meditation, Mindfulness or What I Call Less-mind-ness

(Because we need to reduce the number of thoughts and the amount of thinking we do!)

Meditation is the ultimate way to make time for you and is the biggest act of self-love and self-care. It also benefits you in many ways, including increasing your self-confidence.

Purposes of Meditation

- Relax the body.
- De-stress and reduce tension.
- Quiet the mind.
- Focus the mind.
- Become more aware.
- Awaken creativity.
- Obtain answers.
- Become more intuitive.
- Receive inspiration.
- Connect with your Higher Self.
- Realise your Oneness.

Benefits of Meditation

- Creates calmness and confidence.
- Has a positive effect on the immune system.
- Slows down the ageing process.
- Aids concentration.
- Increases stamina and vitality.

- Lowers anxiety levels.
- Has a positive effect on memory.
- Creates a feeling of inner contentment.
- Reduces blood pressure.
- Increases potential.
- Gives you a feeling of connectedness.
- Makes it easier to experience the Oneself.
- Helps to discover your purpose.
- Increases self-love.
- Raises your vibration.

Present Moment Release

This is one of the ultimate ways to discover the art of being present, has a profound calming effect on people, pets and the environment you are in and is the one I personally use for myself and when I am with my horses and my clients. It literally can be done anywhere (perfect for waiting in a long supermarket queue) and with your eyes open! Perfect for the busyaholic!

Wherever you are, get very still in your body. Shoot roots into the ground from your feet and connect to the Light from above. Focus on the ground you are standing on and notice if it is even, hard or spongy. Next, put your attention on everything else you can feel. Your shoes, your clothes, the temperature of the air surrounding you. AT THE SAME TIME as you are feeling everything, tune in to all the different sounds you can hear; near and far. Maybe the planes, the cars, the refrigerator, your breath.

At the same time as you are feeling and hearing, notice what you are seeing. However, instead of looking around, place your focus on one thing but notice what you can see to the top, bottom, left and right. Usually, everything will be in a softer focus. You can extend this to include what you can taste and smell, but what you can feel, hear and see are the most essential senses. Now you can't stop your thoughts, but you *can* stop getting into a conversation with them. For example, you might have the thought 'There is someone talking near me'. Going into thinking and conversation with that thought would be 'I wonder what they are saying? Are they going to come towards me?' Instead, just acknowledge that thought, then focus back on what you can feel, hear and see. After about a minute, come back to where you are.

A tip I was given that I follow is to set your alarm every hour. A quick minute re-centring yourself, connecting to Source and releasing worry will pay dividends.

There are lots of different ways to meditate. Find the way that works best for you.

Finally

For years, Jerry always believed and told herself she didn't have time to meditate. One reason was that she had the belief that you had to sit crossed-legged for at least an hour and that would have been painfully impossible for her.

Another reason was that, being addicted to rushing around led to her tell herself that the hour meditating would be an hour she could use to get other things done from her ever-growing, never-decreasing to-do list. Such is the insanity of addictions.

Jerry admitted it was an intimate connection that was lacking. Just like having superficial conversations with friends and not sitting down and going into a deeper level of communication, she was afraid to really express her feelings, her fears, her joys, her gratitude and even her tantrums! Hence her addiction to busyness.

After life events brought her to her knees, she allowed herself to overcome her fear of intimacy with Source and learned how to surrender her defiant will, which had just kept slowing her life down. Since she handed over the direction of her life to be guided daily, asking, 'Who do you want me to serve?', 'What do I need to do next?', 'Show me how to live my perfect life', her life has taken off. She is doing more of what she absolutely loves, she is receiving abundance at a whole new level and her self-confidence has increased in leaps and bounds. She is no longer caught in the addiction of perfectionism and procrastination, but she is creating her perfect life.

> *When you **own** the **now**, you have **won**.*
> —WENDYISM

For your free bonus content go to www.imperfectasiam.today

CHAPTER 11

Finding the Perfect Solution in the Imperfect Situation

Having the Courage to Fail
Gives you the Confidence to Succeed.
—WENDYISM

By now, if you have been implementing the suggestions along the way through this book, instead of continually beating yourself up for things not going 'right', you are kind and loving to yourself and others. You have raised your vibration to see beyond your old stories and beliefs. If you are now willing to allow yourself to make 'mistakes' (or 'outtakes in the movie of life', as I call them), you will come to realise how that *builds* your confidence rather than *destroys* it through the harsh judgement of yourself as not being good enough or being useless or stupid.

This gives you far more courage to move forward in your life. Everything no longer must be 'perfect' because there is perfection in everything. It takes away the need to try to control everything and everyone, and so you will gain a wave of inner peace and calm that sees you through any seeming life challenge with tenacity and strength.

No failure now, only feedback. Your strength becomes infectious. The courage to be your authentic self shines through. Now discover how you can use your seeming failures, dramas and life events — not as stumbling blocks, but as springboards to catapult you forward. In each experience of adversity, there are always hidden gifts, and your journey through this book has given you clues, guidance and direction on how to find the perfect solution in the imperfect situation.

> *Failure is unimportant.*
> *It takes courage to make a fool of yourself.*
> —CHARLIE CHAPLIN

The Perfection of Failure

If you need extra inspiration, or more understanding of how failures became successes, then read the stories of people like Walt Disney, Oprah Winfrey, Steve Jobs, Richard Branson, Madonna and Abraham Lincoln, to name but a few. None of them had it easy; none of them had perfect lives or upbringings.

Thomas Edison is famous for his thousands of experiment 'failures' before he found success.

'The electric light has caused me the greatest amount of study and has required the most elaborate experiments', Edison wrote. 'I was never myself discouraged, or inclined to be hopeless of success'.

Remember you are not the first person to fail, make a mistake or not be perfect, and you will not be the last. The quicker you can let go of the need to avoid making mistakes at all costs or needing 'perfection in everything', the quicker you can get on with your life, doing what really matters.

Exercise: How to Deal with 'Failure' (AKA What I Call 'My Life's Research'!)

Step 1.

Go through the emotion, event, failure or mistake which causes you to react. This is vitally important because this is one of your buried feelings (from past events) that needs to come out to be healed, e.g., 'I've failed to get this perfect, and I am afraid others will reject me because of it and this is causing me to feel hurt and afraid'.

Step 2.

Hold on to that emotion and track where in your body you have been storing it and for how long. Ask yourself, 'If I were to remember when I first felt this, it was probably at the age of _____'. Trust the first number that comes up, e.g., 'I was ten years old, and I have been storing it in my stomach'.

Step 3.

Now ask yourself, 'If I were to guess what was going on, it was probably _____'. e.g., 'Dad leaving me'.

Step 4.

Emotions are caused by beliefs, so what is the belief that is creating that emotion? Think through that memory. What are you saying to yourself about yourself or the situation? Or what is the assumption? e.g., 'I feel hurt and rejected, therefore there must be something wrong with me. I am not good enough'.

Step 5.

What was the need not being met? e.g., 'Being loved and accepted and reassured that nothing was wrong with me'.

Step 6.

How can you give yourself that need *now*? e.g., 'I need to love and accept who I am unconditionally. I need to reassure myself I am good enough'.

Step 7.

How will that change the situation you are in? e.g., 'I can lovingly reassure myself that it's just a mistake and I can rectify it. No big deal!'

Step 8.

Make the changes or adjustments.

Step 9.

Rinse and repeat until you get the outcome or success you are seeking!

One of my amazing clients, RK, offered to share her story of how she took several failures and turned them into successes.

The Pain of Pretending to Be Perfect

It was a warm night in late spring of 2017. I woke up in a cold sweat. My heart was pounding so loud that I was afraid I might have a heart attack. I couldn't breathe. With shaky hands, I reached for my inhaler. Usually, I would be able to breathe normally again in less than a minute. But this time, my shortness of breath seemed to worsen. I took two more puffs and waited. No signs of improvement. When I realised the inhaler wasn't helping, I got scared. I was all alone. My husband was travelling for work that week. The sound of my pounding heart seemed to get louder and louder. My hands were clammy with sweat and my breath extremely short and difficult. I felt like I was burning up. I was certain I was either having a heart attack or about to die of a bad asthma attack, so I called the emergency services.

A few hours later I was in the Accident and Emergency Ward of my local hospital, being told that what I had experienced was a severe panic attack. Whilst I was glad that my heart was perfectly normal, I was very unhappy and confused to hear that I had probably never been asthmatic. All the symptoms pointed to undiagnosed anxiety and depression caused by prolonged workplace stress. This had been going on for at least six months!

Flashback to July 2016

A new manager. Something felt amiss. My gut told me to be careful. But my head told me to trust her if I wanted to be accepted. And so, I went with my head — as I had always done in my career. Being a woman, and of brown skin, I had always believed that I needed to make an extra effort to belong. Over the eight months that followed, I tried to be the perfect employee. I took on large projects and delivered great results. I took on tight deadlines and managed complex situations. I even implemented programmes of work that totally went against my personal values. But for me — most important at the time — I had to be perfect and compliant.

I have always been a person who goes the extra mile — and have been rewarded for it. In this case, however, it seemed that the more impactful I was, the more aggressive *both* my superiors seemed to become towards me. Whilst the feedback from my business clients was positive, the feedback from my superiors continued to get worse and worse. I couldn't understand why. My manager's manager — who was known to be abusive in nature — would speak to me unnecessarily loudly, cut me off mid-sentence and command me to think in certain ways.

Every time I met with her, I left feeling belittled and insulted. But I never said anything. I dared not. I wanted to be accepted and liked. It was more important to me than anything else. But all my attempts at being perfect seemed to make things worse! One day in October, at a meeting that became confrontational, I broke down. After that day, I found myself forgetting small things. Missing meetings. Not being able to function properly. I found that I was exhausted all the time. I could not sleep for more than four hours — and even that was interrupted with frequent nightmares. I felt as though I had emotionally and mentally 'checked out'.

Finally, in February, after a terrible clash with my manager over my performance, I realised she had been manipulating and backstabbing me. I also learned that other senior leaders who could have stood up for me chose not to say anything, fearing repercussions. After all, HR was extremely powerful. All these realisations that day led me to have a full-blown panic attack. I never went back to that job again. I was burnt out.

Initially, I felt very confused. After a twelve-year-long successful career, how could I have let this happen? How could I have failed so badly? I had tried to be so perfect — where had I gone wrong?

A few months later, during that summer, horses entered my life. I started Wendy's HEART Equine-Assisted Therapy. My first sessions were all extremely difficult. Every single horse I worked with seemed to physically push into me. I had to physically push them away and found it extremely difficult. I didn't want the horses to dislike me. I wanted to be polite, but in return they'd just push harder into me. As the sessions continued, I began to discover that it was only when I'd allow my true submerged feelings of anger, fear and sadness to show that the horses responded. I felt so vulnerable and exposed, yet at the same time it gave me the courage to push the horses back out of my physical space. They finally stopped pushing into me.

With every next session, it became clear — the horses were teaching me how to stand up for myself, speak my truth and protect my boundaries!

At the end of that summer, I came to realise what I had been doing 'wrong' that had led me to burnout. I was trying to be perfect for everyone else. I also came to see that I had been treating myself as harshly as those bosses, and that had to change first. What Life needed from me was to stand up for *my* truth, *my* values, *my* boundaries AND, most importantly, be kind to myself.

In August 2017, I acquired my own horse and started an Equine-Assisted Coaching business. My experiences with horses and humans continue to challenge my boundaries and values. When you are around horses, you discover that they don't look for you to be polite or perfect. They don't look for you to comply. What they need from you is 100 percent authenticity. When you act and speak according to what you truly value and believe, they sense that congruence between your thoughts, feelings, energy and your physical body. Only then will they BELIEVE you and TRUST you.

It became perfectly clear to me that year.

All my life, I have adapted so that I can fit in. I had tried to be perfect for other people's ideals. It worked. I was accepted. However, the point had arrived where I could no longer get away with leading my life according to other people's values. It was now time to embrace the next stage of my evolution and live by *my* values and *my* truth.

The intention was set. Frustratingly, behavioural change can take longer than we want it to. Whilst I could now see what I needed to do in certain situations, I still found myself doing the opposite. I still said 'yes' when my gut wanted to say 'no', and I kept quiet when other people crossed my boundaries — then I would explode later. I still did not live from my inner truth 100 percent. I still needed to be perfect and accepted.

It was only when I had a very serious horse-riding accident in 2018 (I broke my leg) that something deep inside me shifted. It had to! I was stuck with a metal frame around my leg for six months. Pain humbles you. It makes you go deep within. And so, I did. I realised that I had to make an active choice.

Either I could wallow in my pain and misery and become even more depressed than I had become in my last job (be a victim), or I would use the opportunity to STOP completely and dig deeper to find my truth (be a player). Again, the horses in my life inspired me to seek deeper.

> *Horses have a way of inviting you into a realm of pure consciousness. And when you connect with them there, you connect with your own deepest truth.*
>
> —RK

In the months that followed, during my recovery, my truth became clear to me. I realised that I had many strengths and values that I had been trying to hide my entire life so that I could be nonthreatening and pleasing to others around me. I realised that from early in my life, I had formed the belief that all the negative emotions I felt were bad, and I felt guilty for feeling them. I had formed the belief that I was a bad person who did not deserve to be loved. And yet, the need to be loved was intrinsically always there, and that kept driving me to 'over-adapt' and try and be perfect. Deep down inside I believed that if I were to honestly be my true self, nobody would love me.

So, life brought me a job with manipulative bosses, horses and a broken leg. I had to learn how to step into my truth, love myself for who I truly am and live life from a place of celebrating my authentic self.

Fast Forward — October 2020

This year has been fabulous. I have lived it 100 percent according to my values and, because of this, I have attracted work that has been rewarding and fulfilling. Colleagues and partners with shared values have come into my life. I have been able to make a positive difference in the lives of a few hundred people through the coaching and teaching work that I do and often by sharing lessons from my personal story. I allow myself to be vulnerable — and it feels much more honest and truthful than trying to be perfect. My relationship with myself is one of authenticity. I recognise, acknowledge and celebrate my values. When they are pushed into, I push back. (As taught by the horses!) I honour myself and my ecosystem. I am humbled to have this awareness and feel rich and powerful to be achieving the potential that God/Universe gave me! I can honestly say I am genuinely happy now!

I have learned that there is no point in 'seeking perfection' because I am already perfect as I am and have always been so. Somewhere in my childhood, I was told otherwise and started to believe it. And somewhere in my thirties, Life saved me by requiring me to see and be otherwise.

Today, I feel excited about starting a fabulous new full-time job again — something I would never have dreamed possible after my burnout. I had become so resentful towards working in an organisation and being employed by somebody else, believing that I needed to adapt and be perfect to fit in. Today, I have learned that 'fitting in' is no longer as important to me as 'bringing my unique value to'. And I can only do that now because I finally know what makes me unique. I celebrate it. I love it — all of it. And I believe that so long as I continue to live from my place of truth, authenticity and love, I'm perfect as I am.

Thank you, RK. Your journey is so inspiring and has been a privilege for me to be part of.

RK's story epitomises that all the 'failures' she had courageously been through gave her the confidence to succeed — but now in a much more authentic way.

Exercise: Taking Back Your Power

Take a moment to reflect on where you are giving away your power to people by pretending you are perfect.

How have you been afraid to stand up for yourself in the past?

How can you start being more authentic now?

How can you step through the risk of rejection and speak your truth?

Where can you now allow yourself to have the courage to fail so that you can gain the confidence to succeed?

When you allow yourself the feedback of failure,
you create the opportunity to succeed for sure.
—WENDYISM

For your free bonus content go to www.imperfectasiam.today

CHAPTER 12

The Tasks Before You Are Never Greater Than the Power Behind You!

The purpose of living is living your purpose—wholeheartedly.

—WENDYISM

One of the biggest challenges for most people today is to be humbly proud of who you are and lead an authentic life that isn't governed by unrealistic expectations of perfection, whether that be of your body, your home, your work or other areas of your life.

From a self-image perspective, the knock-on effect we are noticing is that there is anorexia on one side of the pendulum and obesity on the other. Anxiety, depression and other mental illnesses have been on the rise due to social media pressures, especially among the younger generation. Addictions have increased in myriad forms. Yet, is what we are seeing just a 'plague' of lack of self-love and a fear of not being good enough that has created an epidemic of feeling 'imperfect' instead of recognising 'I'mperfect as I am'?

What Is Your Why?

The way to take charge and reach true fulfilment is to have a purpose and find your why. Your why is your reason to live. Your why is the reason you have chosen your career. It doesn't have to be huge, e.g., a global mission, but it *does* ideally have to feel bigger than you. You really do count, and you really do have a unique purpose on this planet. You have a combination of gifts absolutely like no other. You are a unique being, a 'one of a kind', in the same way that every snowflake and grain of sand has its own individuality.

Yes, there may well be other people doing what you do. But this Universe has created you like no other person, to deliver YOU and the gifts you are able to give in your own special packaging.

> *If you can't be you, you can't be anyone else.*
> *They've all been taken, in case you haven't noticed.*
> —WENDYISM

Look at how many authors there are. There are billions of books in existence. Yet something drew you to the message in this one, and although not unique in concept, it certainly is in its delivery, style and content. Your life purpose could use the energy of perfectionism (and procrastination) that has been focused inwardly on yourself (and is all about you and your ego's needs) and turn it outwards to help someone else's life become a bit more perfect for them.

Your talent as a perfectionist (i.e., the ability to see what is wrong all the time) presents you with the perfect skill for a career that needs that special eye. This 'eye for excellence' replaces the pain of nothing being perfect enough. Spiritual psychologist Chuck Spezzano suggests an empowering self-mastery tool to use when you are in pain: 'Think about who needs your help. When you can stop making it about you and make it about them, your pain will dissipate'.

This doesn't mean going into sacrifice and the avoidance of dealing with that pain, but it does mean being of service to others. This is where you gain a true sense of self and can truly accept yourself just the way you are. I hasten to add this doesn't mean you will give up wanting the best, looking your best and having the best things in life. It's being your best self that is no longer desperately needing absolute perfection in the way you look or behave for fear of rejection or appearing not good enough. You are no longer seeking perfection to get the approval of others.

You have your power back. You have true self-esteem, self-worth and self-confidence. More importantly, you emanate authenticity, which has far more integrity to it than creating 'the lie of perfection' and living the illusion of a perfect life.

Your Life Purpose Becomes Your Divine Purpose

What do we mean by purpose? Your purpose is a feeling of why you are here on the planet. What have you to offer that is uniquely special? It doesn't have to be big and global; something more local is just as valuable. It could even be being a parent. Your Divine Purpose is not just something you do; it is something you are. Living your Purpose is sharing your gifts you came here to give. Instead of trying to *get* love, joy or peace, you are the *expression* of love, joy, and peace. Your energy field emanates those qualities through your work, your family and your home. People only have to think of you to sense your gifts.

Your Divine Purpose allows you to surrender your will and plans for happiness and instead let yourself be guided by the Intuitive Power within you. Now you will see *true perfection* in your life.

Everything that is needed to create that Divine Purpose comes to you in magical ways. It doesn't mean you won't meet challenges or difficult people along the way, but now you can trust that everything you are going through is perfect and right. The perfect right people come into your life to help you get to the next level.

About a year after the fire, we were getting back on our feet, and I was ready to employ someone to help me in the office, a luxury I hadn't been able to afford before. After interviewing several people and knowing exactly what I needed, I hired this amazing, perfect PA (I'll call her 'Sandra').

Sandra immediately got stuck into the filing and organising and even had us all spring-cleaning the office and reception! Finally, we had structured systems in operation, and I was thrilled at my 'manifestation'. Sandra was incredibly thorough and checked everything fully. She was a perfectionist.

Sandra had been working for about a month when I noticed murmurs of discontent from other members of staff and customers. I brushed off their concerns as 'a new brush sweeps clean' and explained we needed to embrace change. I didn't even want to contemplate whether I had made a mistake in my choice. Meanwhile, the little niggles started within me. There seemed to be an increase of conflicts going on with the staff, and even some of the horses were getting a bit agitated. I ignored my gut feeling.

More Challenges

Nearly every day, Sandra would inform me what was wrong with other members of staff, and she stated that she could do their jobs as well, so I could get rid of them. Fortunately, most of my staff had been with me a long time and I was very loyal to them, so I dismissed her claims.

By then I had a very uneasy feeling, yet still I didn't want to act on it, as I desperately didn't want the effort of finding another admin person. But life has a way of pushing you to deal with stuff or people you don't want to, and eventually, after a big argument over refusing to sack someone on her say-so, I sacked her instead. If only that were the end of it.

Whilst I was working away in Scotland (which Sandra was aware of), my yard manager suddenly had several visits from various authorities:

the RSPCA, the local licensing authority, the Riding School Approval Centre. In addition to this, my vet, my insurance company and other significant people all received letters telling them we were doing things wrong and that there were welfare issues with the horses. This was the ultimate way to upset me to the core, since my entire life has been dedicated to the care and welfare of horses.

I was devastated. My whole life's purpose was in question, my reputation, my business, my horses, my competence. Sandra was trying to have my business shut down. How dare she? Rage erupted in me.

> Conflict without = Conflict within
> —WENDYISM

I thank God — literally and regularly — for my having learned about the metaphysical workings of the Universe, and especially for my understanding of the Law of Reflection. This law shows you exactly that what is on the inside of your mind will appear on the outside. In other words, what *you* love, hate, believe, fear about yourself, others or life will be *perfectly* reflected by the people you meet, the feelings you are going through and the situations you find yourself in. I had to find this part of me that Sandra was mirroring. Now, outwardly, of course, I didn't want to sabotage my business and close it down, but I had to find the part of me that inwardly did. 'Do you want your business or not?' a stern part of me asked. What was my internal conflict that was causing so much conflict, chaos and confusion externally?

On the Edge

I was staying in this stunning house sitting on the edge of Loch Lomond. I stared at the still waters. 'Why do you want to destroy everything you have worked for?' I solemnly asked myself. I allowed myself to feel the deep pain, anguish and anxiety I felt at the possibility of the horses having nowhere to go. 'How on earth am I going to feed them?' The dread in my stomach was sickening. My thoughts went to the children, clients and staff who would be let down. It was unbearable. I felt such shame for cocreating this stressful situation for everyone by my choices of staff hire and other poor business decisions. I sobbed and sobbed and then sobbed myself to sleep. All I could do was surrender.

A New Dawn

When I woke up, I felt a strange calm come over me. I had reached many conclusions and realisations. I had found the part of me that DIDN'T want the business anymore. BUT it wasn't *all* the business I didn't want; it was just certain aspects of it: the over-responsibility, the physical hard work, the admin side. They were all taking my energy away from being able to focus on what I absolutely loved doing — my HEART Equine-Assisted Therapy, writing and spiritual coaching. I had been feeling resentful of my energy being pulled in loads of different directions and not being able to centre myself on doing what I truly loved to do.

I took myself through several of the exercises I've already shared with you in this book and cleared the buried feelings and emotions, changed my beliefs that 'I have to do it all', 'I never have time for me', 'I shouldn't be allowed to run a yard because I am not good enough' and many other self-attacking thoughts, and set about putting into action what I WAS going to do about the situation.

I recommitted to my business but was determined to put new boundaries and support in place. I used the energy of rage I had initially felt and turned it into reigniting the passion for my work.

The upshot was that the enquiry from all the 'authorities' proved unsubstantiated, and nothing was taken further. They all realised this was just a disgruntled staff member trying to cause trouble. However, I secretly knew it was the perfectionist part of me that was always telling myself I wasn't good enough, wasn't doing it right and that I didn't deserve to run a business.

A few months later, we had our 'proper' annual Local Authority inspection and, ironically, because of Sandra, our paperwork was perfectly in place, and this was instrumental in our attaining the new 5 Star Award, the highest in standards. The Universe really did send me the perfect right person at the right time, which helped me, my purpose and my business evolve to a whole new level.

When you follow your heart and your sense of purpose, you attract the right support at the right time, providing you believe that you deserve support and getting your needs met. Now you may be wondering how on earth Sandra could have been the perfect person I needed. In truth, if I hadn't had that major wake-up call, I would still have been living a half-life. Sandra was perfect for me on so many levels. I had to get very clear about my business, I had to make serious changes; she had inadvertently taught me how to get the business side organised with her attention to detail and that helped (as previously stated) to get that 5 Star accreditation. I was also able to employ the right staff to help me with those parts of the business I struggled with. By allowing myself to trust the process, I could allow the Universe to finally help direct my life and business.

Perfection

I'm sitting here, ironically, back up in Scotland again. I am on my last few days here at the Isle of Skye Trekking and Therapy Centre, delivering my HEART Equine-Assisted Coach training to a wonderful group of students who are just about to take their final assessment before being awarded their diplomas. I am bursting with pride at how far they have come, and I am bursting with pride for myself. I am on the last few words of the last chapter of this book.

I have a wonderful new yard manager and several trustworthy staff deftly supporting the care of the horses in my absence. I have the most dedicated office manager. They all constantly go over and above. They are doing what they love; I am doing what I love: writing, creating courses, delivering my HEART Equine-Assisted training programmes and online courses. I have the most amazing herd of horses which bring so much joy, healing and transformation to so many people. I have incredible clients who support us continually with their business, even through the restriction of lockdowns due to the pandemic! I have the most amazing business partner, who is my extraordinary wing-woman, and last, but not least, I have the most wonderful husband, who lovingly supports me unconditionally to do what is true for me. To me, that is true perfection.

Thank you, God, for always bringing me perfect right people, in perfect right timing and perfect right situations. I surrender my life to your will and guidance.

It's now two years on from when I first started the book at sixty-two. I haven't shed all my sixty-two pounds' excess weight yet, and only half of the sixty-two projects are completed. There are hundreds of things that need improving in my life. I am still a work in progress. But all in good time.

The difference is that I am genuinely happy with who I am now. I have cleared my debts, my business is flourishing and I am enjoying an amazing abundance of money, vitality and energy. I finally love who I am, as I am. I am no longer trying desperately to prove I am good enough, worthy enough or deserving of my life going well. I am now free from my self-imposed prison, and I have a whole new level of self-love, self-acceptance and self-confidence. I now believe myself when I say I'mperfect as I am. I can finally trust that I am always divinely supported and truly know that everything has worked and is working perfectly.

Thank you for your time reading this book. I trust it has given you some fantastic ideas and that you too can now also say 'I'mperfect as I am' — and believe it.

*The purpose of living is to remember your connection
to yourself and Source, and that you are one
with everything and everyone, of course.*
—WENDYISM

P.S. All my students passed their exams with flying colours!!

For your free bonus content go to www.imperfectasiam.today

Made in the USA
Columbia, SC
08 April 2022